# AMERICAN COUNTRY FOLK CRAFTS

# AMERICAN COUNTRY FOLK CRAFTS

**50 Country Craft Projects for
Decorating Your Home**

Carol Endler Sterbenz

Photography by Beth Galton

In Association with

McCall's
NEEDLEWORK
&CRAFTS

Harry N. Abrams, Inc., Publishers, New York

**For Margaret Gilman, who knows
"It isn't easy being green."**

PROJECT MANAGER: Lois Brown
DESIGNER: Darilyn Lowe
DIRECTIONS WRITER: Eleanor Levie
PATTERN ILLUSTRATOR: Roberta Weiss Frauwirth


**Library of Congress Cataloging-in-Publication Data**

Sterbenz, Carol Endler.
    American country folk crafts.

    "In association with McCall's needlework &
crafts."
    Bibliography: p.
    1. Handicraft—United States.   2. Folk art—
United States.   I. Title.
TT23.S74   1987          745.5          86–32095
ISBN 0–8109–1857–9

Times Mirror Books

Printed and bound in Japan

# Contents

# Introduction

I love quilts—old and new—and it was because of my passion for them that I began to explore and to appreciate the history, tradition, and craftsmanship of American handwork.

As a crafts designer, I have always been interested in knowing how something is made, and once I know, I am often inspired to try my hand at creating a personal version. I discovered that the more I knew about folk crafts, the more I wanted to know and to try for myself. Through designing crafts and collecting old pieces, I began to see America from the perspective of the craftsman; I realized that in the coverlets, hooked rugs, folk paintings, wood carvings, portraits, and weather vanes, I was reading a text of our American social history. At the same time, I was gaining direct access to the creative imagination of the individual artist whose work I was examining, and I knew that every folk craft evolved from the wellspring of creativity.

*American Country Folk Crafts* is a tribute to and celebration of that creative process which is manifest in design native to America—design by and for the common man that is unencumbered by formal rules and techniques, design that possesses clarity, directness, and wit. *American Country Folk Crafts* draws on the fiercely independent spirit of the American colonists and the early pioneers, and it speaks the language of sweetly fragrant new-mown hay, icy-cold water from an outdoor pump, and rows upon rows of tiny quilting stitches. This personal collection of American folk crafts is inspired by American country living and all the values it embodies. Though this book is primarily a collection of folk crafts that I have personally designed, the settings include antique folk art from private collections, as well as fine examples made by craftsmen working today. The kinship in this book between past and present folk crafts is obvious and intentional; there is a shared sense of history as today's folk artists continue to follow the tradition of making things by hand, one by one, no two works exactly the same, and all works having one thing in common—the spirit of America.

Ranging in difficulty from elementary to advanced, the craft projects consist of such techniques as sewing, embroidery, crochet, quilting, rug hooking, woodworking, wood carving, paper cutting, painting, and some baking. Complete step-by-step instructions and patterns can be found in every chapter. *American Country Folk Crafts* is totally accessible to those who want to bring American Country into their homes and certainly will motivate even the beginner to try a number of the projects. And of course there are contemporary craftsmen across the nation producing works that embody the spirit of the folk-craft tradition, and the names and addresses of a good number of these people from whom you can purchase folk crafts can be found in the "Directory of Craftsmen" at the back of the book.

I hope you will enjoy and use *American Country Folk Crafts;* it provides an opportunity to take part in, first hand, the creative traditions that are distinctly American. This Country collection is presented in several homes where folk crafts unify and enhance the domestic interior. Each house was chosen for its inherent strengths, as well as for the context it could give the featured crafts. The photography, the supporting text, the directions and patterns, and the "Directory of Craftsmen" combine to provide many levels of access to the handmade of America. Whether you just feast on the visuals, or you are inspired to create a folk craft of your own, you will be sharing the original craftsman's journey down a now historic path.

*Carol Endler Sterbenz*

# The Dining Room

**BIRD NAPKINS**
**LEMON MOUSSE NESTS**
**MINCEMEAT PIE**
*SCHERENSCHNITTE*
**SILHOUETTE**
**FRAMED QUILT BLOCKS**
**SAMPLER**

The American Country style, of course, is more than an assemblage of folk art—antique or contemporary. Room settings are personal statements about our tastes, our collecting loves, and our lifestyles. Country is a way of life. It is fresh flowers and vegetables, home-baked cakes and pies and breads, a relaxed atmosphere that includes space for active children and pets, and neighborliness. My husband, John, and I enjoy informal entertaining and one of our favorite times is Sunday afternoon. The noon meal has settled, the children are sequestered in their rooms finishing homework; it is a special time to gather with good friends and to linger over some homemade delight and fresh-brewed coffee. I like to say welcome by fussing a little over the table setting and baking something from scratch. Over the years, I have collected recipes for hearty breads, cakes, and pies. I prefer to rely on tested recipes from experienced bakers who are willing to share hints and secrets. Coming from a home of craftsmen, not cooks, I appreciate hand-holding in the kitchen.

A mincemeat pie recipe given to me by a master in the kitchen, Vermont homemaker Mrs. Robert W. Berard, is a special combination of ingredients that includes green tomatoes. It is delicious! The pie will be served in the dining room of a painstakingly restored 18th-century Vermont farmhouse. The plates are authentic Quimper ware. The 1870 pine table from New England has a distressed look from years of use. The chairs are black-painted, bow-back Windsor armchairs. Hand-forged antique silver rests on handmade fringed napkins embroidered with a blue-outline type of handwork that depicts a variety of stylized birds. These birds were inspired by the popular mid-19th-century stoneware crocks that are decorated with cobalt-blue slip birds. (Outline work from the 18th and 19th centuries was usually done in red, with tight stitches at evenly spaced intervals; red outline work can be found on old table linen, and less frequently on bed linen.)

Behind the table is a wall with waist-high wainscotting painted white. Hanging above is a rather realistic depiction of a country road in spring. The bright palette, the painterliness, the perspective, and the realism of this painting suggest the work of a schooled artist, though it is unsigned. By contrast, the folk artists of past centuries did not represent their subjects realistically. These folk painters, who traveled from town to town, were called limners. They were self-taught and usually developed a personal style. When these itinerant painters were asked to do portraiture, they were expected to communicate the social standing of the subject rather than to capture the person's particular physical characteristics. As a matter of fact, many Southern aristocrats commissioned portraits by mail. It was not unheard of for an itinerant painter to receive a letter from a client describing the land and objects he possessed, as well as detailing his standing in the community. Paintings had a sliding-fee scale based on their size as well as on the amount of detail and rendering. A portrait or landscape always cost more if there was "shade." However, to ensure an adequate income, limners had to paint more than portraits. Many began as craftsmen and had developed a varied repertoire of services. They hand-lettered coffin plates and painted decorations on furniture and carriages. To make portraiture accessible to the more rural, less sophisticated clientele, limners created cut-paper silhouettes. Termed the "poor man's miniature" (two profiles cost 25 cents), silhouettes could be "hollow cut." In this technique, a light-colored paper is cut out following the contour of the person's profile; the hollow-cut is then placed over a dark background, with details like ringlettes and collars added afterward in watercolor. Portraits could also be made by utilizing the cut-out silhouette. This profile is applied to a background paper or cloth, and then glazed to preserve its delicate condition. Placed prominently in the home, these sentimental "renderings" were available to and desired by most families.

A lovely antique silhouette is shown on the tea table (page 21). The bust-length profile of a young woman with a bonnet and dangling ribbon at the nape of her neck is a graceful portrait created in the 19th century by a Long Island, New York, limner. Preserved in an oval frame, the silhouette is from a collection of portraits of a Long Island family. One can imagine the limner asking each member of the family, in turn, to be seated between a lighted candle and a piece of rag paper attached to a wall, and then painstakingly drawing, snipping, and mounting each profile. Unfortunately, with the advent of the daguerreotype in 1840 this quaint art lost favor.

However, the expression of sentiment is still supported by other romantic traditions. One such tradition comes from the Pennsylvania Germans. It is called *scherenschnitte*, which means "scissor cutting" in German. This folk craft involves folding and cutting white rag paper into intricately designed love tokens or valentines. Given all year round to express longings of the heart, these cut-work valentines are embellished with intertwining hearts and doves; flowers and vines are applied carefully with watercolor; the lacey-cut portions are inscribed with poetry, and frequently they are further decorated by dipping a hand-wrought pin into ink and pricking a design along the "arms" of the cut paper.

Created in the same spirit of past centuries, my "Tree of Life with Hearts and Doves" scissor-cutting is a contemporary response to the *scherenschnitte* tradition. Circular in overall form, with four tree trunks breaking into leafy branches as doves and hearts rest peacefully, a hand-inscribed, stream-of-consciousness prose winds around the intertwining boughs creating another design element. Placed on a blue background to bring out the intricate cut work and the watercolor design, this valentine hangs in the dining room below another charming example of early American handwork—the sampler (page 20).

The Frances A. Clapp sampler, dated 1836, is named for its creator. Frances was twelve years old when she stitched it. Originally, samplers were made by young girls in order to practice the techniques of mending, darning, decorating, and monogramming. As the student learned new patterns and motifs, she kept a record by stitching them, randomly placed, on a foundation fabric. These samplers were kept in sampler boxes or trunks and added to by the stitcher as she learned her art. Later they were used as a reference when she assumed the tasks of repairing and embellishing the family clothing and linen. By displaying samplers in the parlor, proud parents could discreetly exhibit the talents of their unmarried daughters for prospective suitors.

Another needle art required for young ladies was quilting. Patterns and specific techniques were passed from mother to daughter. When mother was quilting, the daughter would sit beside her and practice the tiny, even-running stitch required in the construction of any quilt, and if the hands of a novice did not produce a work of art, still every stitch refined her needle-and-thread skills. These skills were viewed as a social asset. The early 1800s saw gatherings where quilters contributed their own personally designed patchwork squares and their unique "signatures" to a friendship or album quilt. Quilting was indeed a "penmanship," and those whose work was filled with irregularities found themselves without invitations to quilting bees. Quilting lore has it that long ago there were two spinster sisters who, after scrutinizing the day's quilting, closed their shutters and ignored the knocks of callers in order to requilt an entire coverlet which failed to meet their perfectionist standards of workmanship.

I am afraid that the two quilt blocks which I chose to frame would have caused a similar reaction. However, I was charmed by their unpretentious naiveté and reminded of the broad spectrum of workmanship in collective quilts. Every quilter did not produce a magnificent creation. The value of a quilt was certainly acknowledged immediately upon completion, and the best ones were protected from the sunlight and laid out only for special guests. However, certain humble patterns done in an untrained hand remain a source of delight to me. These affectionately pieced antique quilt blocks are simple geometrics (page 24). The block to the left is the Nine Patch pattern and the one to the right a variation of the Pieced Star, composed of four squares of eight triangles, bordered on their interior sides by narrow strips. The chairs are Queen Anne and the fine wood carving is of an American eagle.

Certain occupations and crafts were passed from father to son, apprentice fashion. Such was the case with glassmaking—one of the first industries in early colonial times. A broad windowsill in Virginia Gray's Long Island, New York, dining room is a lovely place for her collection of clear, pink, and green antique American glass. The pretty and delicious lemon mousse in meringue nests is her creation. This dessert is quick and easy to make, and perfect for drop-in guests.

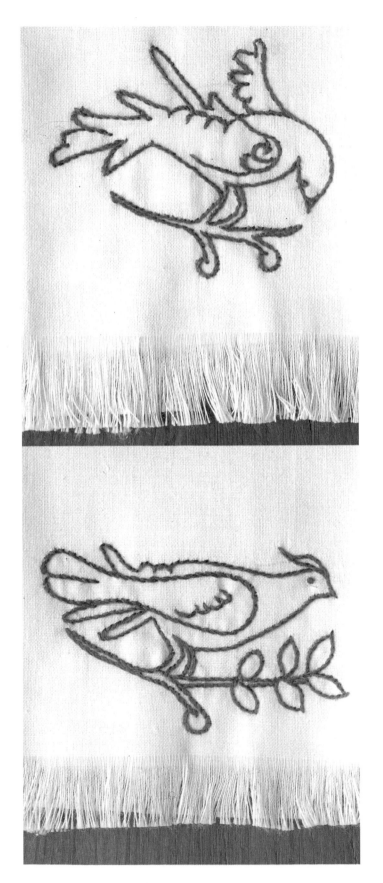
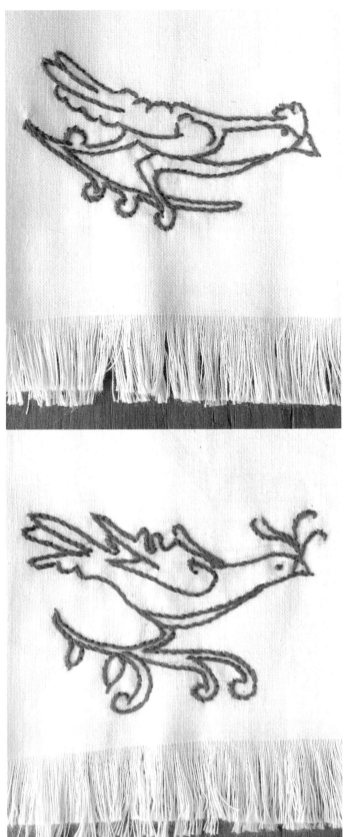

ACTUAL-SIZE PATTERNS FOR BIRD NAPKINS

# Bird Napkins

*Size:* 12" × 16".

*Materials:* For 4: White, finely woven cotton or linen fabric 36" wide, ¾ yd. 1 skein Wedgwood Blue six-strand embroidery floss.

*Directions:* For each: Cut a 12¼" × 16½" rectangle along grain of fabric. Trace lines of bird design, shown actual-size in photographic detail (page 15), onto tracing paper. Pin design to center of one 12¼" edge, with bottom of branch 1½" from raw edge. Insert dressmaker's carbon paper ink side down underneath, and transfer design lines with a sharp pencil. Separate floss and use 3 strands in an embroidery needle to embroider lines in tiny stem stitches; refer to "Embroidery Stitch Details" on page 151.

*Finishing:* Pull out thread to fringe raw edge along embroidery for ¾". Hem remaining edges by turning under ⅛" twice to wrong side and slip-stitching. Press from the wrong side.

# Basic Pie Crust and Lattice Top

2 cups all-purpose flour
1½ teaspoon granulated sugar
1 teaspoon salt
¾ cup plus 2 tablespoons vegetable shortening
¼ cup ice-cold water

*Directions*

1. In a large mixing bowl, combine dry ingredients.

2. Cut shortening into dry ingredients and mix until corn-meal consistency is reached.

3. Add water, drop by drop, mixing with fork until mixture leaves sides of bowl.

4. With hands, form a ball; divide dough in half. Refrigerate.

This recipe will make two 10-inch pie crusts or one 10-inch pie crust and a lattice top.

*Pie Crust Bottom*

Place one ball of dough on pastry cloth; roll until approximately ⅛ inch thick and over 10-inches in diameter. Fold in half and place over half the 10-inch pie plate; unfold so pie plate is covered.

*Lattice Top*

Place ball of dough on pastry cloth; roll a rectangle approximately ⅛ inch thick having a measurement of 12 inches on its longest side. Cut long strips of desired width. Weave the strips, one at a time, while strips are on top of pie filling. Crimp ends onto bottom pie crust using a fork or your fingers.

## Lemon Mousse Nests

*Meringue*
4 egg whites
2 teaspoons lemon juice
1 cup sugar
2 tablespoons lemon rind

Preheat oven to a low 200 degrees. Line baking sheet with wax paper.

Beat the egg whites until frothy. Beat in lemon juice and slowly beat in sugar until stiff peaks form. Fold in lemon rind.

Fill pastry bag (fit with a plain tip) with the meringue. Pipe small circles onto the baking sheet. Build up the sides of each meringue by piping an outer ring on top of each circle. Bake in a low 200-degree oven for 1½ hours or until dry. Let cool before pouring in lemon mousse filling.

*Lemon Mousse Filling*
1 envelope unflavored gelatin
¼ cup cold water
4 egg yolks
¾ cup sugar
½ cup lemon juice
1 teaspoon lemon rind
1 cup heavy cream
2 kiwi fruit

Soak gelatin and water together. Combine beaten egg yolks, ½ cup sugar, and lemon juice in a double boiler. Cook over boiling water until smooth and thickened, stirring constantly.

Remove from stove; add gelatin and stir until dissolved. Add lemon rind and chill until just beginning to set (about 5 minutes). Beat 1 cup heavy cream until soft peaks form; beat in ¼ cup sugar. Fold whipped cream into the lemon mixture. Fill each meringue. Let set in the refrigerator for at least 1 hour. Peel and slice kiwi and place on top of each meringue.

# Mincemeat Pie

2 pounds green tomatoes
1 teaspoon salt
½ lemon
1 orange
1 tart apple
½ cup seedless raisins
1 tablespoon vinegar
½ cup brown sugar
⅛ cup sweet cider or apple juice
⅛ teaspoon cloves
⅛ teaspoon nutmeg
¼ teaspoon cinnamon
pinch of ginger

### Pie Crust
*To basic pie crust recipe on page 16, substitute lard for vegetable shortening.*

Preheat oven to 450 degrees. Line a 10-inch pie plate with one unbaked pie crust; press gently to sides and bottom.

Chop tomatoes, discarding stem area; sprinkle with salt; let stand 2 hours. Drain tomatoes and place in a large enamel pot; cover tomatoes with boiling water and let stand another 10 minutes. Drain.

Seed lemon, orange, and apple; chop and add to tomatoes. Mix remaining ingredients into tomato mixture and cook over medium heat, stirring occasionally, for 1 to 1½ hours, or until mixture is thick.

Let mixture stand 1 hour and then pour into pie crust. Form lattice top as described on page 16. Bake at 450 degrees for 10 minutes; reduce heat to 350 degrees and continue baking for approximately 40 minutes. Cool.

# Scherenschnitte

**Size:** Paper cutting, 8½" in diameter; framed, 11½" square.

**Materials:** Sheet of typing paper. Cartridge pen with permanent brown ink, or fine brown felt-tip marker. Watercolor paints: blue (1), rose (2), ochre (3), aqua (4), olive green (5), and tan. Colored mat board. Craft glue.

**Equipment:** Tracing paper. Stapler. Graphite paper. Small, sharp scissors. Straight pin. Small paintbrush. Mat knife.

**Directions:** *Transfer Pattern:* Trace actual-size quarter pattern onto tracing paper. Cut typing paper into an 8½" square. Fold horizontally in half, then vertically in half again, following Diagrams 1, 2, and 3. Open last fold. Place quarter pattern over right side of paper, matching centers and dash lines of pattern with fold lines of typing paper. Staple along edges to secure. Insert graphite paper carbon side down in between, and place another sheet of graphite paper carbon side up, underneath all layers. Go over all lines and fill in all blackened areas with a sharp pencil, pressing firmly so as to transfer pattern markings to two quarters of the typing paper. Remove pattern, turn it to the back, and go over lines so they are easily seen from this side. Place this side of pattern over left half of typing paper, matching edges and centering carefully; transfer as before.
*Cutting:* Keeping the typing paper folded horizontally in half, staple the three open sides together along the filled in areas. Blackened areas show what will be cut away. Fine lines indicate areas to be painted—do not cut these areas.

Working through both layers, use the tip of the scissors to pierce a hole in any interior filled in areas, then carefully cut out along outlines. Carefully unfold paper. Check to make sure bottom half is cut neatly, and make any additional snips necessary to ensure this. Place piece under a heavy book to flatten, or press gently and briefly with a dry iron.

*Painting:* Paint areas within fine lines by number: referring to materials list, paint bird blue, flowers rose, ochre, or aqua, and all leaf shapes olive green. Dot birds' eyes with a darker shade of blue.

*Inking:* Use pen to mark details. Outline flowers and aqua flower centers, birds' beaks. Write verses in a flowing script as follows, or as desired: Start at one heart and work around clockwise. Slashes indicate a new line. Heart #1: My/ Dearest/ Should fortune cast/ its gaze on me/ and bless me with/ sweet works/ from/ thee … Heart #2: Pray, give me pause,/ these works impart/ a friendship, dear/ from deepest/ heart. Heart #3: Perhaps, true friend-/ ship can aspire/ to grander heights/ that you/ inspire. Heart #4: How sweet the music/ of your name/ My life will/ never/ be

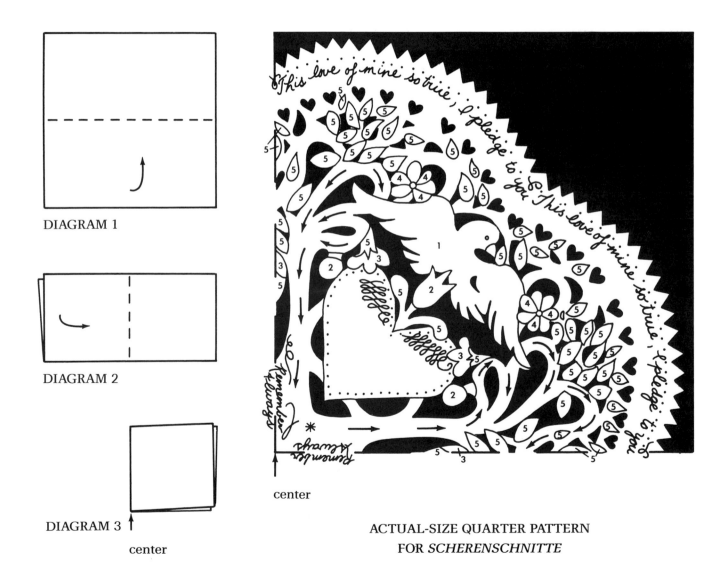

DIAGRAM 1

DIAGRAM 2

DIAGRAM 3

center

center

ACTUAL-SIZE QUARTER PATTERN
FOR *SCHERENSCHNITTE*

19

the/ same. Fill in any remaining empty spaces with scrollwork, as shown on pattern. Make tiny dots all around hearts, just inside cut outline.

Snake the following love letter along loopy tree branches. Start at the asterisk (*) on one of the quarters and follow the arrows around; slashes indicate the start of a new loop, to help you pace yourself so prose just fills the available path: When upon life's path I travel I think of you./ You are a light . . ./ You are a joy. You are the words on my lips./ The symphony of my soul./ The utterance of my heart./ You are mine./ How dear this life of mine with you to share/ to touch/ sweet love divine . . ./ cherish/ I know that I shall never want nor ask for/ more than your faithful heart. I pledge my friendship./ I pledge my love, fair one, whose heart love pierced by Cupid's bow. I hope that it was long ago when first we met where roses grow/ and delphiniums/ and asters and fragrant clusters of lilac/ just beyond the meadow/ where the field meets the garden fence.

At the center of the paper cutting, write "Remember Me" in script. Repeat "Remember" in all directions and add "Always". Along each outside curve of the paper cutting, repeat "This love of mine so true I pledge to you."

*Pin-pricking:* Using a pin, pierce tiny holes all around outside edge.

*Finishing:* Using a mat knife, trim the mat board to an 11½" square. Use a pencil and ruler to lightly mark 8" lines horizontally and vertically across the center. Turn the finished paper cutting to the wrong side. Apply very small dots of glue along the center and at regular intervals all over; use only a minimal amount of glue. Place the paper cutting glued-side down onto the board, matching centers and aligning fold lines with penciled lines on mat board. Press down firmly and let dry. Frame as desired; use glass to protect piece.

ACTUAL-SIZE PATTERN
FOR SILHOUETTE

## *Silhouette*

*Size:* Approximately 5″ in diameter, framed.

*Materials:* Tracing paper. Graphite paper. Thin black paper such as origami paper or flint paper. Cream-colored paper. Spray adhesive. Semi-gloss varnish. Small, sharp scissors. Round 5″ frame, with easel stand.

*Directions:* Trace silhouette, shown here actual size. Center tracing paper, wrong side up, on back of black paper. Insert graphite paper in between and go over outline with sharp pencil, to transfer. Remove pattern and graphite paper. Carefully cut out silhouette.

Cut cream paper to fit inside frame. Spray adhesive on back of silhouette, and adhere to center of cream paper. Apply two thin coats of varnish, letting piece dry after each coat. Set into frame.

# Framed Quilt Blocks

**Size:** Each, 9½" square, framed together, 22" × 12".

**Materials:** Small amounts of cotton fabrics: For Block 1, red pinstripe and blue-and-white check; for Block 2, white sailcloth and blue baby gingham. White sewing thread. Frame with 12" × 22" opening. White matboard. Fabric glue.

**Directions:** Read "General Directions for Quilting" on page 152.

*Quilt Block 1 (Nine Patch):* From red pinstripe fabric, cut five 3½" squares (A). From blue check, cut four 3½" squares (B). Arrange as shown in assembly diagram. Stitch squares together in rows, then stitch rows together.

*Quilt Block 2 (Pieced Star):* First cut joining strips along grain of white fabric: one 1½" × 9½", two 1½" × 4½". On graph paper, draw a 2" square. Divide square diagonally in half. Glue resulting triangle to cardboard for template. Use template to cut 16 triangles from both white (A) and gingham (B) fabrics. Stitch a white triangle to each gingham triangle along their long edges to form squares. Place 4 squares together as shown in diagram for 8-patch square. Stitch squares together in horizontal rows, then stitch rows together to form 4 ½" squares, including seam allowance all around. Lay out quilt block: for top row, place 2 squares on flat surface with short joining strip in between. Place long joining strip below for row 2. Repeat top row below that, but rotate squares a quarter turn so that a B patch is at upper left corner; refer to photograph (page 24). Stitch squares and joining strips together in top and bottom rows, then stitch rows together.

*To Frame:* Cut mat board to fit frame. Arrange quilt blocks, evenly spaced, on top; dot backs with glue to secure. Frame with glass.

|   |   |   |
|---|---|---|
| A | B | A |
| B | A | B |
| A | B | A |

ASSEMBLY DIAGRAM
FOR QUILT BLOCK 1

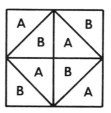

ASSEMBLY
DIAGRAM FOR
8-PATCH SQUARE IN
QUILT BLOCK 2

# Frances A. Clapp Sampler

**Size:** About 14″ square.

**Materials:** Zweigart's 22 count Hardanger cloth, beige #13, 20″ square piece. Six-strand embroidery floss, 1 skein each color listed in color key, unless otherwise indicated in parentheses. No. 24 tapestry needle. Sewing thread.

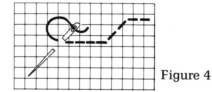

Figure 1

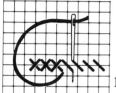
Figure 3

Figure 2

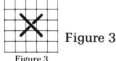
Figure 3

Figure 4

Star Stitch

**Directions:** *Prepare Fabric:* To prevent fabric from raveling, bind raw edges with masking tape. Fold fabric horizontally and vertically in half, and baste along fold lines to mark center. Using a sharp colored pencil, draw center lines following arrows on chart, to correspond with basting on fabric. Work design counting out from center guidelines on chart and fabric.

Work embroidery in a hoop; move hoop as needed. Cut floss into 18″ lengths; separate strands and work with number of strands indicated for each chart. To begin a strand, leave an end on back and work over it to secure; to end, run needle under 4 or 5 stitches on the back. For all charts, refer to color key for colors. For main chart, each square on chart represents 2 fabric threads. Work cross stitches over 2 horizontal and 2 vertical threads, using 2 strands of floss. For verse and age charts, each square represents 1 fabric thread. Work cross stitches over 1 thread in each direction, using 1 strand floss. Begin first word of verse by counting down from the letter "g" in last alphabet row, as shown. *Note:* Diagonal symbol represents a half-cross stitch to complete comma, not a color change. For vowels chart, follow arrows on chart to center row of vowels between side borders; leave 7 fabric threads blank between upper border and top of alphabet. Each symbol on vowels chart represents a star stitch; see stitch detail. Use 2 strands of floss.

When embroidery is completed, steam press lightly from the back. Frame as desired.

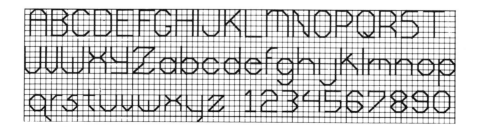

25

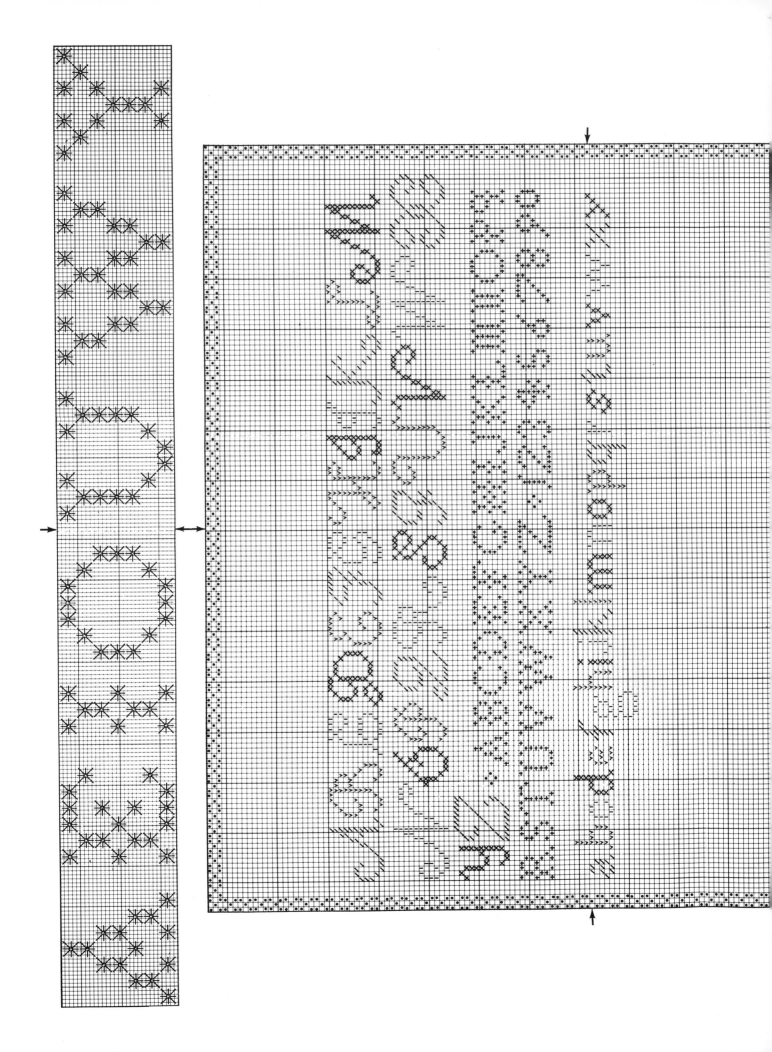

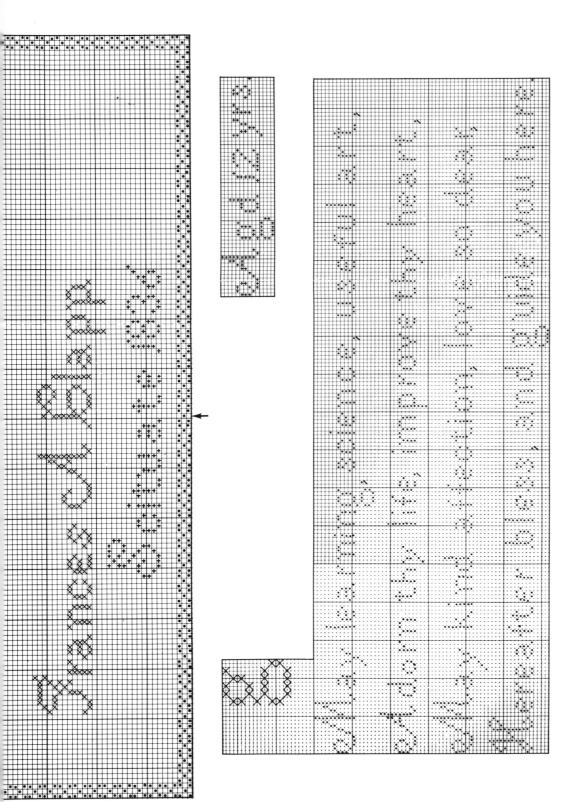

| COLOR KEY | | DMC # | ANCHOR # |
|---|---|---|---|
| ● | Dark Blue (2) | 930 | 922 |
| ✗ | Medium Blue | 931 | 921 |
| ✚ | Light Blue | 932 | 920 |
| ◢ | Terra Cotta | 356 | 5975 |
| ▼ | Olive | 3012 | 843 |
| Ⅱ | Amber | 435 | 369 |

# The Kitchen

CHERRY/APRICOT/PINEAPPLE PIE
APPLE PIE
OLD-FASHIONED CHERRY PIE
APRICOT/PINEAPPLE PIE
HORSE & HEART HOOKED RUG
BARNYARD ANIMAL PARADE
CHICKEN IN A BASKET
FREEHAND WALL PAINTING
COUNTRY FRIENDS DOLLS
MAMMY DOLL
HEART PILLOWS

The country kitchen with its fireplace providing heat and light was the family gathering place in the houses of 17th- and 18th-century American small towns and settlements; often it was the main room if not the only room in the house. The fireplace was constructed with a brick oven so that the homemaker could bake and cook indoors. Built to serve many purposes, the early American country kitchen contained the dining table and chairs and also the beds, as separate sleeping rooms did not develop until much later. It is ironical to note that today's homes have many rooms, each related to a distinct function, and yet, when guests visit, everyone gravitates to the kitchen.

The word "kitchen" has always meant very special things to me. I have wonderful childhood memories, especially around Christmastime, when my sisters and I would bake scrumptious cookies, or when we would clear the kitchen table and paint our own Christmas cards. I can still smell the fragrant cinnamon sticks floating in my parents' brew of Christmas wine, and I can still hear the hammering of the radiator as heat was sent up the pipes. It was not a fancy kitchen, but it was comfortable and accessible.

I found another accessible kitchen in a Massachusetts barn that had been converted into living space. Originally a wide "hall" that ran between a cart shed and the threshing floor of the barn, this kitchen has an enviable atmosphere of country warmth. Saw-cut cupboards and shelves are painted a soft yellow ochre, as are the walls and window trim. Long drawers secret away loom-woven towels and place mats, cutlery and silverware. Stacks of nested copper lusterware (with a rare and beautiful pattern), Can-

29

ton china, and ironstone platters rest on the open shelves of the cupboard. The eclectic country feeling is reinforced by the accumulation of kitchen utensils, cookware, and antique baskets collected and hung on the wall above the sink, most within easy reach.

The phrase "as American as apple pie" was coined to reflect the abundance and popularity of the apple, as well as to identify the perfect solution for its utilization. Though the early homemaker was responsible for a myriad of household tasks, she nevertheless found ways of expressing her creative imagination. If washing and cleaning restrained it, baking unleashed it. Presented here is an intricately latticed pie crust covering a cherry/apricot/pineapple filling, which was created by Vermont homemaker Wendy Girardi. Garnished with dried apricots, a cherry, and periwinkle leaves, the delicate lattice strips trellis the tangy mixture inside. The bolder lattice strips of Mrs. Berard's apple pie cover the still-warm fruit baked inside. These pies sit on the shelf of a cast-iron stove made at the turn of the century (page 32). Still working, this cast-iron stove also baked a marvelous old-fashioned cherry pie. Created by Linda Kundla of Long Island, New York, it is another example of the simple but sublime possibilities with basic ingredients. Wendy's lattice-work apricot/pineapple pie is cooling on a *paradenhantuch* (page 35).

On the floor by the cast-iron stove is an oval, multicolored braided rug. These rugs were popular throughout the 18th and 19th centuries in rural America; they were made by braiding long, wide strips of wool into long ropes which were then coiled and stitched together. The wool had been salvaged from worn clothing and household fabrics. Though homey, these floor coverings are limited aesthetically. By contrast, there are many pattern possibilities if one chooses to hook a rug. Hooked rugs are made by pulling narrow strips of cloth, usually wool, through a burlap foundation (although linen and hemp were used prior to the mid-1800s). The most durable rug resulted when the hooked loops were close together. A sparsely hooked rug, however, did not usually indicate poor workmanship as much as it suggested the scarcity of materials in the scrap bag.

Early hooked rug patterns were derived from embroidery designs and some were inspired, if not copied, from Oriental carpets. There were, of course, the many homemakers who simply took charcoal and an empty grain sack, and drew their own primitive designs. These freehand designs were often charming and whimsical. Particularly appealing are the single-animal motifs showing household pets or farm animals. Marion N. Ham of Limerick, Maine, created this traditional hooked rug with the well-loved motif of the horse and heart (page 35). Its near-perfect symmetry is created by hooking mirror images on opposite sides of a framed rectangle. The earth tones are reminiscent of the home-brewed dyes made from available berries and barks, such as woad, sassafras, and pokeberry.

If the aesthetic and functional aspects of a motif or symbol influenced its use and popularity, nowhere is this more in evidence than in folk-art weather vanes. Constructed to provide information about the weather since the prosperity of many towns depended upon the benevolent or malevolent forces of nature, weather vanes also communicated the occupations and pursuits of the owners. Placed high on barn roofs were profiles of running horses, lambs, cows, and roosters; in the coastal areas, where shipbuilding, whaling, and sailing were important, weather vanes boasted ships in full sail, whales, and seagulls. Made from wood, copper, or sheet iron, these weather vanes could be seen for miles atop the barns that stood on the quilted landscape of America.

These same motifs can be found stitched, painted, and carved on a variety of American handcrafts. Inspired by the 19th-century profiles, my parade of barnyard animals is a whimsical testimony of farm life in rural New England. The silhouettes are cut from oaktag and painted to resemble the sheet-iron weather vanes. A thirteen-star flag adds a splash of color to this grouping (page 38).

Less popular as a folk art symbol is the chicken. However, I was determined to make a plump chicken in soft sculpture. Sitting in a coiled vine basket with some added evergreen, this smartly dressed hen evokes sunrise and fresh eggs (page 39).

Since we often think of folk art as objects combining functional and decorative elements, it is pure delight to see the extraordinary freehand painting of Vermont folk artist Linda Allen. With understated elegance and subtle color, and with steady brushstrokes, this purely decorative expression in paint is a beautiful example of art for art's sake. The cascade of flowing vines, broad leaves, delicate flowers, and ripe fruit was applied to a grainy plaster wall on the upper door frame in the kitchen's pantry (page 42). With an intuitive sense of color and design, Linda succeeds in affirming the spirit of the self-taught, itinerant painter of past centuries.

Beginning in the 19th century, parents and educators began to recognize the value of play in child development. Parents took part in making dolls and toys that could aid in role play and activities that would prepare children for their future place in society. Little girls played house and dolls with the most charming rag babies, including black folk dolls as well as white folk dolls. Simple but lovable, my Country Friends are made from fabric taken from the scrap bag, and please note that Mother Cat's patches match her litter of calico kittens (page 43). The Mammy dolls were probably modeled after beloved caretakers, and my Mammy cradles a baby as she might have in some nursery of long ago. With basic rag dolls such as these, little girls learned real skills for the adult world; hence, stitching crude doll clothes prepared them for dressmaking, etc. A simple project for today's youngsters are the darling heart pillows, which also can be used as pincushions.

## Cherry/Apricot/ Pineapple Pie

3 8-ounce cans tart cherries (reserve liquid)
1½ cup granulated sugar
½ cup cornstarch
1 cup chopped dried apricots
1 8-ounce can crushed pineapple
1 teaspoon almond extract
¼ cup butter
1 cup chopped walnuts

Glaze
1 egg yolk
1 tablespoon water

Pie Crust
Prepare basic pie crust recipe on page 16.

Preheat oven to 350 degrees. Line a 10-inch pie plate with one unbaked pie crust; press gently to sides and bottom.

In a medium saucepan, combine reserved liquid from cans of cherries, sugar, and cornstarch; bring to a boil for one minute, stirring constantly. Add apricots, pineapple, cherries, almond extract, and butter. Stir and refrigerate mixture for 30 minutes.

Sprinkle chopped walnuts onto unbaked pie crust; pour refrigerated mixture on top. Form lattice top as described on page 16; mix egg yolk and water for glaze, brush lattice top. Bake at 350 degrees until pie crust is golden brown and filling is bubbling, about 50 minutes. Cool and garnish as desired.

## Apple Pie

8 to 10 tart apples
⅓ cup brown sugar
½ cup granulated sugar
1 tablespoon lemon juice
Pinch of mace, cinnamon, and nutmeg
3 tablespoons butter

Pie Crust
To basic pie crust recipe on page 16, substitute lard for vegetable shortening; add a pinch of baking powder.

Preheat oven to 350 degrees. Line a 10-inch pie plate with one unbaked pie crust; press gently to sides and bottom.

Peel, core, and slice apples; place in large mixing bowl and add brown sugar, granulated sugar, lemon juice, and spices. Mix.

Pour mixture into pie crust and dot the top with butter. Form lattice top as described on page 16. Bake at 350 degrees until pie crust is golden brown and filling is bubbling, about 45 minutes. Cool.

## Old-Fashioned Cherry Pie

1 quart pitted fresh sour cherries
⅛ teaspoon salt
1 cup sugar
2 tablespoons quick-cooking tapioca
1 tablespoon flour

Glaze
1 egg yolk
1 tablespoon water

### Pie Crust

*To basic pie crust recipe on page 16, substitute Crisco for vegetable shortening, and add ½ tablespoon of vinegar and 1 beaten egg in Step 3. (Add additional flour if necessary.)*

Preheat oven to 450 degrees. Line a 10-inch pie plate with one unbaked pie crust; press gently to sides and bottom.

Put cherries in a large mixing bowl; sprinkle with salt; let stand 5 minutes. Add sugar, tapioca, and flour; mix together and let stand 20 minutes.

Pour mixture into unbaked pie crust. Form lattice top as described on page 16; mix egg yolk and water for glaze, brush lattice top. Bake at 450 degrees for 10 minutes; reduce heat to 350 degrees and continue baking for approximately 40-45 minutes. Cool and garnish as desired.

## Apricot/Pineapple Pie

*13 ounces dried apricots*
*2 cups water*
*½ cup granulated sugar*
*2 tablespoons flour*
*¼ teaspoon fresh ground nutmeg*
*1 teaspoon cinnamon*
*1 8-ounce can crushed pineapple*
*1 cup finely chopped walnuts*

*Glaze*
*1 egg yolk*
*1 tablespoon water*

*Pie Crust*
*Prepare basic pie crust recipe on page 16.*

Preheat oven to 350 degrees. Line a 10-inch pie plate with one unbaked pie crust; press gently to sides and bottom.

Chop dried apricots; add water and sugar; pour into a saucepan and cook over medium heat 15 minutes; cool to room temperature. Combine flour, nutmeg, and cinnamon; stir into apricot mixture; add the pineapple.

Sprinkle chopped walnuts onto unbaked pie crust; pour apricot/pineapple mixture on top. Form lattice top as described on page 16; mix egg yolk and water for glaze, brush lattice top. Bake at 350 degrees until pie crust is golden brown and filling is bubbling, about 50 minutes. Cool and garnish as desired.

## Horse & Heart Hooked Rug

**Size:** 29″ × 54″.

See "General Directions for Hooked Rugs" on page 153. Enlarge pattern on paper ruled into 1″ squares. Centermost foursome of hearts are rust outlined in old gold and green/blue tweed. Pairs of hearts on either side of center are blue or blue tweed with old gold. Heart foursomes at side edges alternate burnt sienna, blue/brown tweed, and rust. Hearts around the sides feature blue tweed centers surrounded by rust, then old gold tweed. Horses are each a different shade of brown or brown tweed. Some have manes, tails, and/or legs in a lighter or darker tone, to contrast. For the border, use blue wool in 3 different textures; work in straight lines for the effect of an inner, middle, and outer border.

PATTERN FOR HORSE & HEART HOOKED RUG   Each square = 1″

## *Barnyard Animal Parade*

**Size:** 22¾″ long, animals, about 4½″ high.

**Materials:** Sheet of oaktag, 18″ × 24″. Acrylic paints: brown and black. Wood strip ½″ × ½″ × 22¾″. Dark brown wood stain. Semi-gloss varnish. Miniature flag, approximately 4″ × 6″ on a 10½″ pole. Craft glue.

**Equipment:** Pencil. Tracing paper. Masking tape. Graphite paper. Xacto knife. Paintbrush. Drill with ³⁄₁₆″ bit.

**Directions:** Cut a 22¾″ × 6″ rectangle from oaktag. Trace animals; tape goose ½″ behind sheep, matching straight horizon line. Place design on oaktag rec-tangle, with horizon line 1″ from one long edge of oaktag, and horse's ex-tended front leg 1½″ from left side edge of oaktag. Tape at intervals to secure, then insert graphite paper in between and go over design lines to transfer to oaktag. Remove pattern and graphite paper. Extend horizon line to left and right edges of oaktag. Place oaktag on a protected surface and cut along animal outlines and horizon line using Xacto knife.

Paint cutout unevenly with brown paint; before paint dries, smudge on black paint with finger to create the look of worn spots. Let dry, then paint the back in the same manner. Let dry, then apply 2 coats of varnish.

Drill hole for flagpole 1″ from one end of wood strip. Stain wood strip; let dry. Glue cutout to wood strip; glue flagpole into hole.

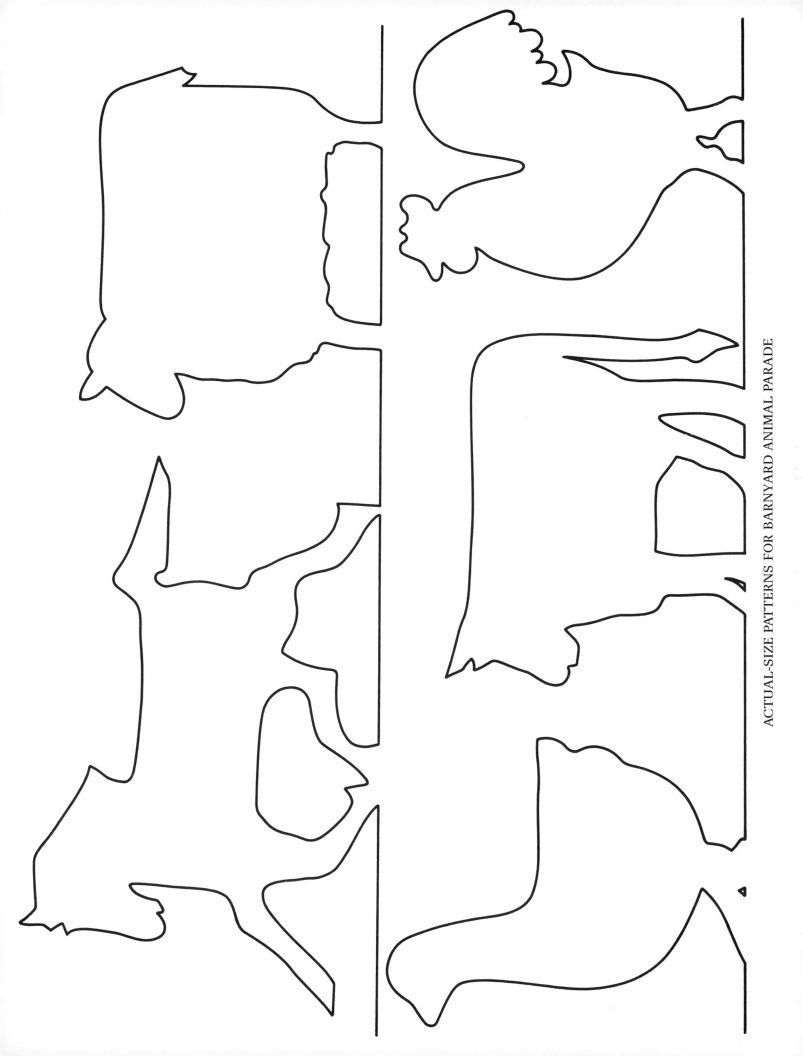

ACTUAL-SIZE PATTERNS FOR BARNYARD ANIMAL PARADE

**Directions:** Read and refer to "General Directions for Stuffed Animals and Dolls" on page 154.

*Enlarge pattern.* Use patterns to cut 2 bodies, 4 wings, 1 rump, 1 underbody from black print, 2 combs and 2 wattles from red print, 1 beak from yellow. Transfer fine line details to right side of fabrics.

Stitch combs together along all but bottom edge; turn to right side. Stuff plumply and pin along top edge of head, matching As. Pin body pieces together, stitch along breast, from A to B, and along upper curved back, from A to C. Pin fan tail to joined body, matching corresponding D-C-D points. Clip curves, and turn to right side. Stitch along fine lines to define tail feathers; be sure to stop lines of stitching ¾" before raw edge of inner curve. Turn back to wrong side. Stitch rump to fan tail, matching corresponding D-E-D edges. Pin underbody to body along B-D edges. Turn and stuff firmly, starting with fan tail sections. Turn open edges of rump and underbody (D-D edges) to inside, pin, and whipstitch together. Turn under edges of beak along fine lines. Fold crosswise in half and tack to body at top X. Stitch wattles together and gather along dash lines. Tack to bottom X. Pleat each wing toward tips of feathers. Stitch together in pairs along all but center 2" of straight edge. Stuff plumply. Stitch straight edge to chicken body along curve indicated for wing placement, gathering wing slightly to match Fs and Gs. At each open circle indicating eye placement, stitch a French knot using 3 strands of pearl cotton.

# Chicken in a Basket

**Size:** 10½" high, 11" long.

**Materials:** Cotton fabrics, 44" wide: black print, ⅜ yd.; scraps of red print, solid yellow. Sewing thread to match. Polyester fiberfill. White pearl cotton. Round or oval basket, 8"-10" in diameter.

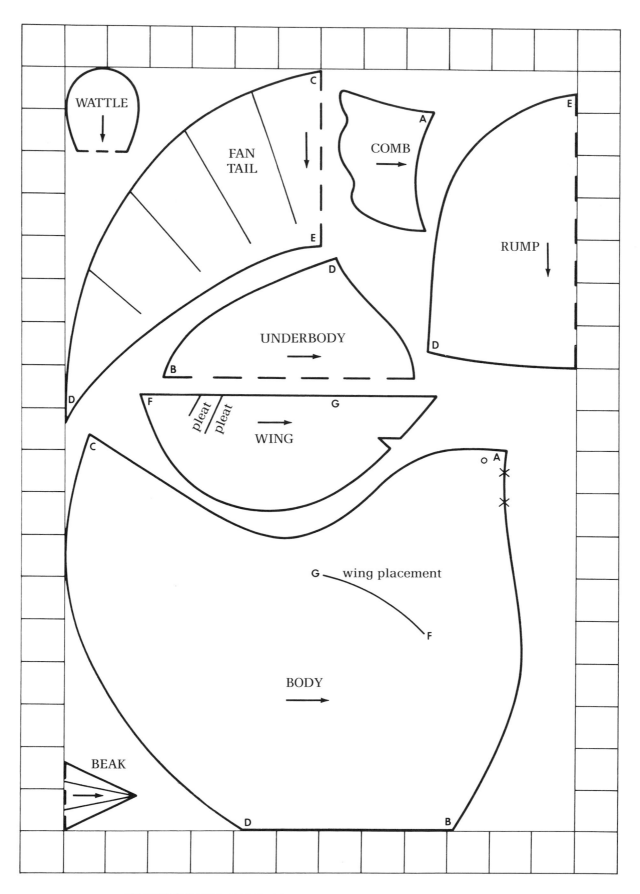

WATTLE

FAN
TAIL

COMB

C

A

E

RUMP

D

D

UNDERBODY

B

F    pleat
     pleat    G

WING

C

o A
×
×

G    wing placement

F

BODY

BEAK

D                    B

PATTERNS FOR CHICKEN IN A BASKET    Each square = 1″

PATTERN FOR FREEHAND WALL PAINTING   Each square = 1"

# Freehand Wall Painting

**Size:** 52" wide.

**Materials:** Acrylic paints in jars: Cadmium Red (CR), Burnt Sienna (BS), Yellow Ochre (YO), Raw Sienna (RS), Burnt Umber (BU), Ultramarine Blue (UB), and Cadmium Yellow (CY).

**Equipment:** Large sheets of tracing paper. Graphite paper. Masking tape. Plastic margarine container. Paintbrushes: round tapered, flat, and fine liner.

**Directions:** *To Make Pattern*: Enlarge pattern on 24" × 30" paper ruled in 1" squares. Trace design, turn tracing to reverse side and line up the 2 half-patterns along dash lines. Center flower is asymmetrical; cut away at overlap to reveal left side, then tape half patterns together for complete pattern.

*Transfer Design*: Tape pattern to clean wall, centering over doorway or positioning as desired. Insert graphite paper, carbon side down, in between pattern and wall; move as needed. Go over all design lines, to transfer. Remove pattern.

*To Paint*: Use lid of margarine contain-

er as a palette. Pour a small amount of paint onto palette at a time. Use bowl to hold water, for diluting paint. To shade, mix colors shown added together (+) only partially, taking some of each pure color and some of mixture on brush.

Practice painting the following brush strokes on a piece of paper. For a teardrop stroke, use round tapered brush; push brush down to its full width, pull it down and gradually lift it so that tip of brush hairs is last to leave the surface. By pulling around instead of down, you achieve more of a comma shape. For an outline, use fine liner brush and thin paint with a little water. Start with tip and slowly increase pres-

sure on hairs of brush; lighten pressure for a fine end.

Refer to color photograph as you work. Using CY and CR, paint flower petals with teardrop strokes. For persimmons (round fruit), use YO and shade with YO + RS. For leaves, use teardrop strokes with UB + CY. Also use UB + CY with outline technique to paint stems, tendrils, and grids at flower centers. For berries, use CR + BS using round tapered brush in a circle; dab on a spot of BU.

If desired, use CR and outline technique to add your initials and date, as shown.

**Country Friends Dolls**

**Sizes:** Girls, 11″ tall, Mom cat, 4″, kittens, 3″.

**Materials:** Cotton fabrics, 44″-45″ wide: *For each girl:* ¼ yd. black sailcloth or beige kettlecloth and plaid homespun-type cotton; contrasting small prints, stripe, or plaid, one 12″ × 18″ rectangle, one 7″ square, small amounts of six others. Thread to match fabrics. Black, white, and red pearl cotton. Pink crayon. Polyester fiberfill. Small wicker basket.

**Directions:** Read and refer to "General Directions for Stuffed Animals and Dolls" on page 154.

*Girl Dolls: For each:* Use patterns to cut 2 head/bodies, 4 arms, 4 legs from beige or black fabric. Stitch pieces together in pairs, leaving the following unstitched: bottom edge and between dots on head/body, short straight edges on limbs. Turn pieces to right side and stuff firmly. Insert arms into body sides between dots, with seams at top and bottom; insert legs into bottom edge of body at corners, with seams at center front and back. Turn open edges on body ¼″ to inside and slip-stitch limbs in place.

*Face:* Using a contrasting color of pearl cotton, stitch a French knot where eye is indicated on pattern (open circle). Sew a red straight-stitch mouth. For beige-skinned girl, rub crayon over cheeks.

*Hair:* Thread black pearl cotton onto embroidery needle; pull ends even for a double strand. Work the following all around head seam at ¼″ intervals: *For black doll,* insert needle through seam; cut pearl cotton leaving 4″ ends. Repeat at same point twice more, for a total of 6 strands. Taking two strands of pearl cotton together, braid tightly for 1″. Cut along one edge of 12″ × 18″ print fabric to make 2 long ³⁄₁₆″-wide strips. Tie a strip around braid 1″ from head, trim strip ends to ½″. Repeat for each braid.

*For white doll,* make a French knot, wrapping thread 4 times around needle each time.

*Clothing: Dress:* Use pattern to cut 2 dresses, 2 sleeves from plaid homespun fabric. Stitch dresses together along sides; hem bottom edge. Clean-finish ends of sleeves. Fold each sleeve lengthwise in half and stitch along long edges for underarm seam. Gather slightly along rounded edge (cap). Pin sleeves, with caps at ends of neckline, into armholes of dress; hand-stitch. Clean-finish dress neckline. Slip dress on doll, and gather sleeve ends and neckline to fit. *Bloomers:* Use pattern to cut 4 from 12″ × 18″ fabric. Stitch pants legs together in pairs along long side seam. Clean finish bottom edges. Stitch inseams. Stitch right and left legs together from center back waist, around crotch, to center front waist. Clean-finish waistline edge, creating a simple casing. Starting and ending at center front, pull white pearl cotton through casing on a needle. Slip bloomers on doll, pull pearl cotton ends taut and tie. *Shawl:* Use a pin to "pick" threads from edges of 7″ square, forming a ¼″ fringe. Fold diagonally in half.

*Mom Cat and Kittens:* Use patterns to cut 2 Mom Cat pieces from one print fabric, plus 2 of each kitten piece from each of 5 or 6 different fabrics. Stitch pieces together in pairs, leaving straight bottom edges open. Stuff firmly. For Mom Cat, cut irregularly shaped 1″ pieces from various fabrics and appliqué randomly: turn raw edges ¼″ to wrong side, pin pieces over surface of Mom Cat, and slip-stitch all around edges. For each kitten's tail, cut a ½″ × 3″ strip from same fabric. Turn edges ⅛″ to inside and fold lengthwise in half, enclosing raw edges; whip-stitch. Insert end of tail at X-mark in bottom corner. Slip-stitch bottom edges closed. (See photo page 43.)

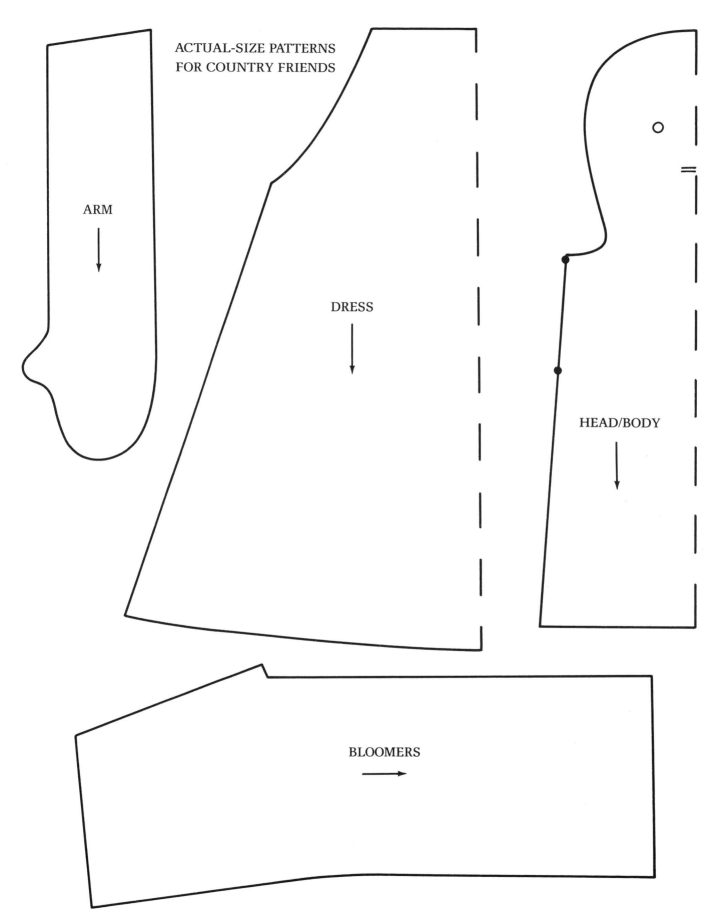

ACTUAL-SIZE PATTERNS
FOR COUNTRY FRIENDS

ARM

DRESS

HEAD/BODY

BLOOMERS

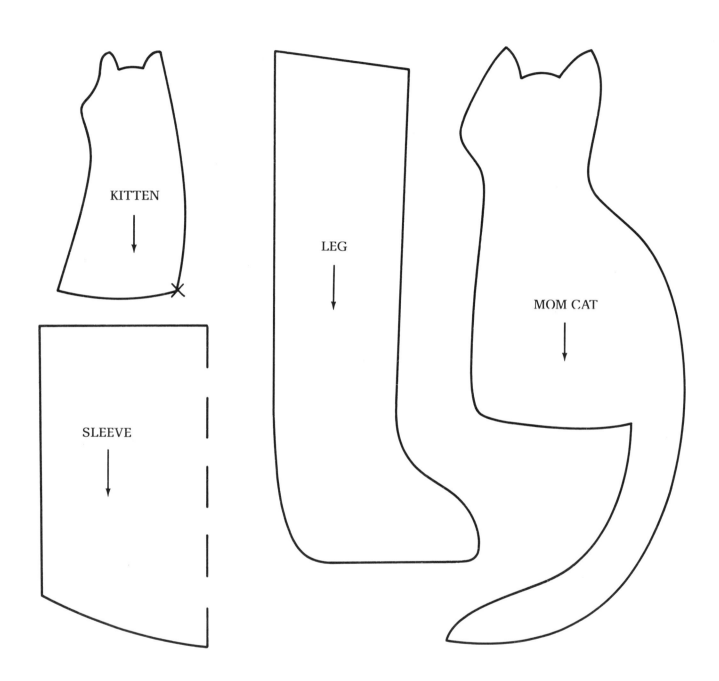

KITTEN

LEG

SLEEVE

MOM CAT

ACTUAL-SIZE PATTERNS FOR COUNTRY FRIENDS

# Mammy Doll

**Size:** 14" tall.

**Materials:** Cotton fabrics: muslin, 36" wide, ⅝ yd.; 12"×18" rectangles each black sailcloth and rust striped print; tan striped knit 60" wide, ⅝ yd.; small amounts of maroon dot and blue plaid homespun. Thread to match fabrics. White quilting (or carpet) thread. Red and white six-strand embroidery floss. Polyester fiberfill. Medium gauge copper wire.

**Directions:** Read and refer to "General Directions for Stuffed Animals and Dolls" on page 154.

*Mammy Doll:* Use patterns to cut 2 head/torsos and 4 arms from black sailcloth. Stitch matching pieces together in pairs, leaving short straight ends of arms, bottom edge of torso, and area between dots unstitched. Turn pieces to right side and stuff firmly to within ½" of openings. Turn edges on torso between dots to inside, insert arms, and slip-stitch together. Gather bottom edge of torso and pull thread ends to close. Embroider face: using all six

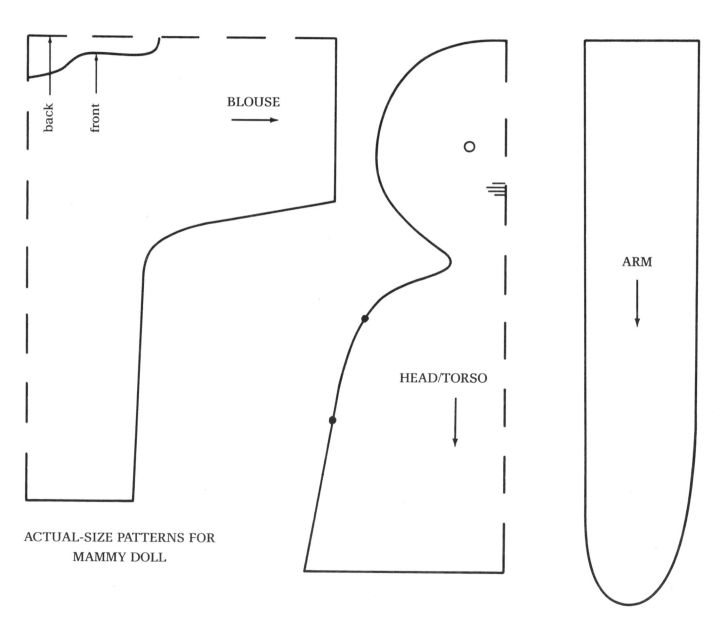

back

front

BLOUSE

HEAD/TORSO

ARM

ACTUAL-SIZE PATTERNS FOR
MAMMY DOLL

47

strands of white floss, make French knots for eyes. Using 3 strands floss in needle, straight-stitch across mouth several times.

*Base:* From muslin, cut a 20″ × 30½″ rectangle. Fold lengthwise in half. Stitch along two short sides and turn to right side. Using pencil and ruler, mark off lines every 1½″ across width of muslin until there are 20 sections. Machine-stitch along all marked lines, creating a series of channels. Omitting one end channel, stuff channels firmly to within 1″ of openings. Bring short ends together, overlapping unstuffed channel, and whipstitch to form a ring. Using quilting thread, gather open end (top) of base, pull thread ends taut and knot securely.

*Assembly:* Perch torso, centered, on gathered edge of base. Hand-stitch all around to secure.

*Dress:* From cotton knit, cut 1 blouse, using pattern; cut keyhole neckline opening at front only. Also cut a 10¼″ × 57″ rectangle, for skirt. With hand-stitching, clean-finish ends of sleeves and neckline. Fold blouse in half along shoulders and stitch sides and underarm seams. Turn to right side. Slip over head of doll; insert arms through sleeves. Tack neckline to doll all around. Tack bottom edge of blouse to bottom of torso at side seams. Bring short edges of skirt rectangle together and stitch. Turn one long (bottom) edge ½″ to wrong side and blind-stitch, to hem. Gather opposite (top) edge, slip over doll's top half to bottom edge of blouse. Tighten and tie off gathering threads. Distribute gathers evenly all around, and slip-stitch skirt to blouse, with raw edges even. *Apron:* From rust striped fabric, cut a 16″ × 10¼″ rectangle and a 1″ × 24″ strip, piecing to obtain length. Clean-finish short edges of rectangle, hem one long (bottom) edge,

and gather top edge to 5″. For waist-band/ties, turn long edges of strip ¼″ to wrong side, then fold strip lengthwise in half; press. Pin center of strip across gathered edge of apron. Topstitch all along strip, securing apron to waist-band. Place apron around doll and tie ends in a bow. *Head Scarf:* From rust dot fabric, cut a 4″ × 18″ rectangle. Press long edges 1″ to wrong side. Place around head, right side out as follows: Tack one end from crown of head to forehead. Leave a 2″ loop and wrap around head, tacking one long edge to fabric at top of head, other long edge to sides and back of head. When you reach forehead again, end off stitches. Tie free end around loop then tuck under to conceal. *Earrings:* Wrap wire around a small knitting needle; let ends overlap for half the circumference, then clip with sturdy scissors or wire clippers. Stitch rings at the center of their overlap to the edge of head scarf at side seams of head.

*Baby:* From black sailcloth, cut a 3″ circle; from blue homespun plaid, cut a 4½″ square. Gather edges of circle, place a ball of fiberfill about the size of a walnut in the center, and pull gathering threads tight to close, for baby's head. For mouth, embroider 2 French knots side by side to center of head; use all six strands of red floss in needle and wrap floss around needle 3 times. Fringe edges of blue plaid square by pulling out threads along edges for ¼″. Place a ball of fiberfill the size of a small plum in the center of the blue plaid square. Place head along the center of one side of square. Wrap all corners toward center of fiberfill ball, tightly encasing ball-body and head. Tack to secure. Tack arms of Mammy Doll to bottom of swaddling blanket, to secure. (See photo page 43.)

# Heart Pillows

ACTUAL-SIZE
PATTERN FOR HEART PILLOW

**Size:** 3".

**Materials:** Scraps of cotton fabric, or quilt fragment. Sewing thread to match. Polyester fiberfill. Potpourri, sawdust, or kitty litter (optional). Tracing paper. Dressmaker's tracing (carbon) paper.

**Directions:** Trace actual-size heart pattern. Glue to cardboard and cut out. Place on wrong side of fabric, ¼" from fabric edges. Trace around with pencil. Marked line is stitching line; cut out ¼" from marked edges, for seam allowance. Place on same or coordinating fabric, right sides facing. Stitch along marked line, leaving 1½" unstitched along one side. Clip into seam allowance along curves and corner; turn to right side. Stuff firmly with fiberfill; if desired, fill center with potpourri for a sachet or with kitty litter for a pin cushion. Turn open edges ¼" to inside, and slip-stitch closed.

# The Porch

 uintessentially American, the country house porch makes a compelling case for stopping a while to "set." It beckons you to stay five minutes longer to finish reading the newspaper, or to linger and complete one more line of quilting, or to eat supper outside just one more fall evening. How can you resist? The country house porch is a way of life and a bridge between yesterday and today.

I had the pleasure of sitting on this timeless country porch in Vermont. I arose early one morning during my stay, grabbed my coffee and my quilting project—a Dresden Plate pattern—and sat with the long-unfinished quilt on my lap, thinking I would stitch a few lines on the plumes placed around the center medallion. I love this quilt with its elegant appliqué pattern, but I did not quilt a stitch! I simply enjoyed the sunshine, the fresh air, and the company of Spike, the homeowner's dog.

The Dresden Plate pattern has been popular throughout the 19th and 20th centuries and requires both pieced and appliquéd quilting techniques. It is a romantic pattern of narrow wedges of pastel-colored fabric pieced together to form a medallion, or plate, which is appliquéd to a background fabric. Circles are appliquéd onto the center of the medallion, and its perimeter is quilted with tiny rows of running stitches. Although this quilt does not have any borders, it is possible to add harmonizing strips of pastel prints to illuminate the central motifs.

A painted checkerboard with red-and-black squares rests on the floor of the porch (page 55). This one-of-a-kind antique is sectioned into a playing board and trays on opposing sides for "won" checkers. Although these particular checkers are made from lathe-turned wood, early checkers were sometimes made from walnut shells or sections of dried corn husks.

The abundance of wood as a natural resource is reflected in the occupations and pastimes of many American folk artists. Wisconsin folk artist LeRoy Zeigler echoes the fine quality of early folk carving. Lathe-turned and saw-cut with a whittled stem, this sumptuous watermelon rests on an old butcher's block (page 58). Long associated with hot, humid, and airless days, watermelons have become one of the most popular folk art motifs today and can be found in theorem paintings, stencilings, and hooked rugs. It is understandable: the bold colors, the curved and organic shape, the wit in its conception—ingredients of good folk-art design, in my opinion.

LeRoy has captured the austerity and piety we usually associate with the Pennsylvania Amish in his Quilt Lady, which was carved out of soft wood and painted in the same manner as early primitive pieces.

Wood carvings identified the type of commerce carried on by store owners. A precursor to the painted wooden sign, the Cigar Store Indian represented the tobacco trade at a time when few people were literate and a sign had to be instantly recognizable. These figures stood outside the store—bolted to the ground, or on wheels so they could be rolled inside when the shop closed. Either way, it is evident that their value was known even then. From the colorful bonnet of feathers (which some carvers depicted as tobacco leaves), to the soft fold of his cloak, to the removable tomahawk and bunch of cigars, this Cigar Store Indian by LeRoy would have satisfied the most discerning proprietor.

Among the quilts airing on the side of the barn is the Log Cabin quilt, so named because the narrow strips (two dark and two light) surrounding a central square resemble the construction of early American log cabins (page 63). The central square traditionally is made from red-colored fabric to symbolize the fire in the hearth. This well-used pattern has the distinction of providing a vast number of overall pattern variations, depending upon the chosen juxtaposition of the dark and light sides of the basic Log Cabin block.

# Dresden Plate Quilt

**Size:** Approximately 68″ × 84″.

**Materials:** Cotton and cotton-blend fabrics, 44″–45″ wide: muslin, 10 yds.; 1 green print, 1½ yds. (includes borders), ½ yd. each of 8 other green prints. White sewing and quilting thread. Quilt batting.

**Directions:** Read "General Directions for Quilting," page 152. Each Dresden Plate design is first pieced then appliquéd to a muslin quilt block. Each block is assembled and quilted separately—making this a very portable project—although optional scrolls are quilted in corners of blocks after blocks are joined. A 2″ border of one green print fabric surrounds the finished quilt. First cut lengths for this border: 4½″-wide strips totaling 6¾ yds. in length.

Using actual-size pattern for wedge, make a template and use to cut 40 from each green print fabric, for a total of 360 wedges.

*Patchwork:* Make 20 "rings" of wedges. Piece 18 wedges to form each ring, using 2 wedges from each print and varying prints as you go. First, place two wedges together, and stitch along one long side. Place joined piece flat, turn top wedge over so right side of fabric faces up, and press seam. Add a third wedge to the previous "top" wedge in same manner, stitching, turning, and pressing. Continue adding wedges to form complete ring of 18 wedges. On outer and inner edges of circle, turn under seam allowance of each wedge and press.

*Quilt Blocks:* From muslin, cut forty 18″ squares; set half aside for backing. Pin a ring of wedges to center of each square. Appliqué, slip-stitching around

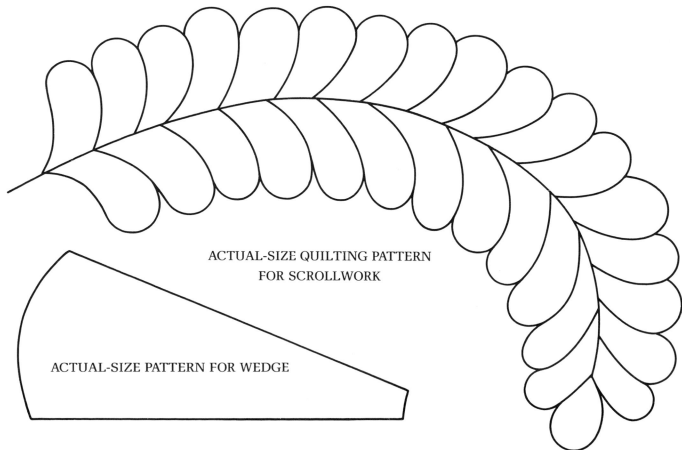

ACTUAL-SIZE QUILTING PATTERN
FOR SCROLLWORK

ACTUAL-SIZE PATTERN FOR WEDGE

inner and outer edges through all layers. If desired, mark blocks for scrollwork quilting: place actual-size pattern for scroll in each corner of block, keeping just 1″ from appliqués and 1″ from edges of block. Transfer, using dressmaker's carbon.

Lay one backing square on work surface right side down, with a same-size square of batting on top. Center quilt block, right side up, on top. Beginning at the center and using contrasting thread, baste out to each corner and to midpoint of each side. With quilting thread, quilt as follows: $\frac{1}{16}$″ to inside of inner circle; along left long edge of each wedge, $\frac{1}{16}$″ from seam; and around entire Dresden Plate motif 4 times, each round $\frac{1}{8}$″ further beyond appliqués. Do not quilt scrolls at this time.

*Assembly:* On a large surface, lay out blocks into 5 horizontal rows of 4 blocks each. Join blocks in each row as follows: Working only through muslin squares of quilt top, machine-stitch with right sides facing and making 1″ seams. Press seams. Turn row to back, then fold back edges of batting and backing to expose seam just made. Trim adjacent batting edges to meet at seam. Join backing blocks as follows: On rows 1, 3, and 5, lay edge of backing square on the left over seam. Turn under edge of square on the right so fold aligns with seam between squares on quilt top. Pin over left edge and slip-stitch in place. On rows 2 and 4, reverse direction of seams, to avoid bulkiness between rows. Join rows together in same manner as for blocks.

Quilt optional scrollwork at this time.

*Border:* Stitch green print strips together. Press one long edge $\frac{1}{4}$″ to wrong side. Stitch opposite long edge to quilt top, right sides facing, edges even, and mitering corners. Turn opposite long edge to backing side of quilt and slip-stitch in place all around.

# Checkerboard

*Size:* 12¾″ × 21½″.

*Materials:* ¾″ pine or plywood, cut to 12″ × 20¾″ rectangle. Wood moulding or firring strips: 1″ × ⅜″ with rounded edge, 6′; ¼″ × ⅜″ with rounded edge, 2¼′. Wood glue. ¾″ finishing nails. Medium oak wood stain. Glossy oil base paint in barn red and black. Varnish. 2 small drawer pulls with screws.

*Equipment:* Masking tape. Hand saw. Sandpaper. Paintbrush. Pencil. Ruler. Tack cloth.

*Directions:* Sand wood board; paint top surface barn red; let dry. Use masking tape to tape off areas 4⅜″ from each short edge. In inside area (12″ square), use pencil and ruler to mark a checkerboard of 1″ squares. Paint alternate squares black, staggering rows; use a straight edge to paint straight and cleanly. Let dry. Stain underside of board.

From 1″ moulding, cut two 12¾″ lengths and two 21½″ lengths, mitering ends. From ¼″ moulding, cut two 12″ lengths. Sand and stain all strips. Glue ¼″ moulding across board at each end of playing area. "Frame" board with remaining moulding strips as shown (page 56), first gluing, then nailing at corners and at ends of ¼″ strips.

Apply two coats of varnish, letting piece dry after each coat. Place drawer pull across center of each end; screw in place.

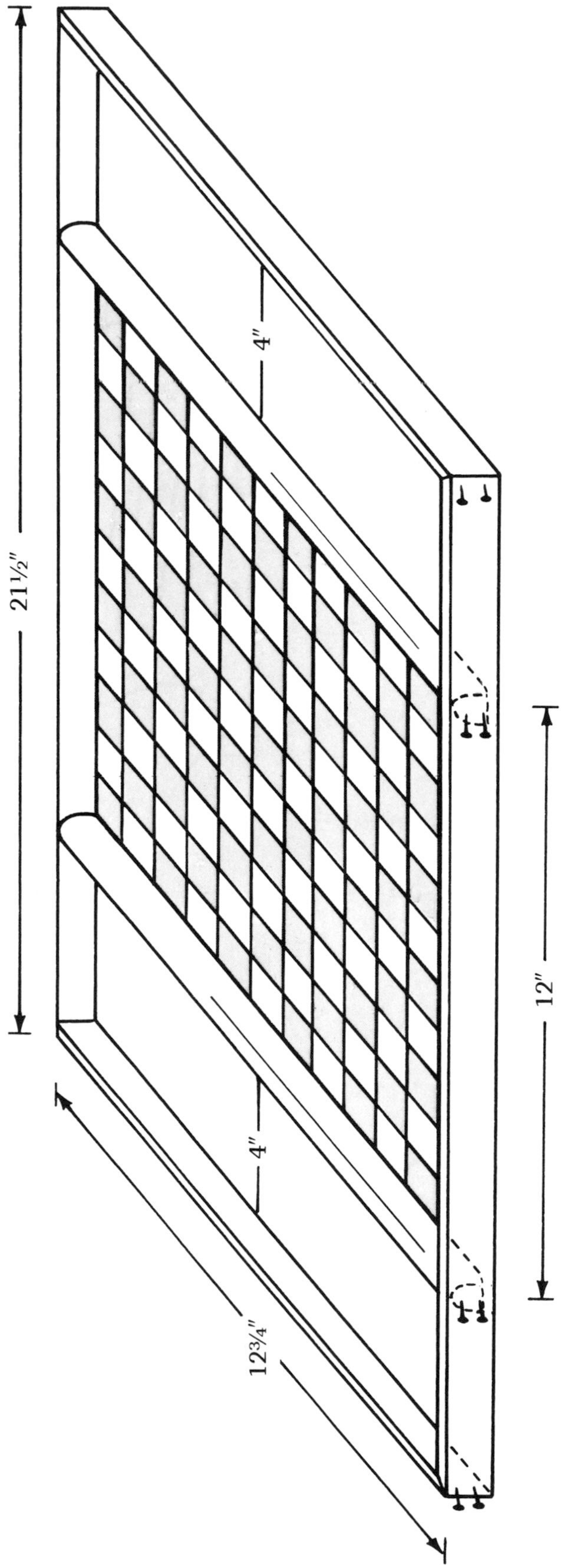

DIAGRAM FOR CHECKERBOARD

21½"

4"

4"

12"

12¾"

# Wood Carvings: Watermelon and Slice, Quilt Lady, Cigar Store Indian

**Sizes:** Watermelon, 13″ long. Quilt Lady, 16⅜″ tall, 18″ with pedestal base. Cigar Store Indian, 23⅝″ tall.

**Materials:** Soft wood such as white pine or poplar. Plastic wood or epoxy putty. Acrylic paints.
*For Quilt Lady:* 2 metal ⅛″ prongs. Glue. Xacto knife.

**Equipment:** Coping saw. Rasps. Several carving knives. Set of chisels. Several grades of sandpaper. Paintbrushes: flat, round tapered, and fine liner.
*For Quilt Lady:* Drill with ⅛″ bit.

**General Directions:** *Prepare panel:* Cut or select a straight-grained block with measurements as indicated in individual directions.
*For Figurines:* Sand all surfaces. Enlarge patterns on paper ruled into 1″ squares. Heavy lines indicate deep cuts; fine lines indicate shallow cuts and painting outlines. Transfer side view image to block. Taking extreme care to line up images, transfer the front image to an adjacent side of block. With band saw or coping saw, cut as follows, 1/32″ outside pattern outlines: Carefully cut out side profile, sawing down the back of the figure, then down the front of the figure, keeping each sawed portion in one piece. Reassemble cut-off pieces with masking tape, then saw out front pattern. Transfer image to back of block. With a rasp, round off square corners. As you carve away design lines of figurines, re-transfer the images.
*For All:* With sharp knives and chisels, begin to carve in overall shape. Cut with the grain whenever possible. Use a gouge to shape concave areas. Move about, doing some work on each section to keep an idea of proportion. Refer frequently to patterns and photos; however, much of the carving has to be done by eye. If your knife or gouge should slip, rebuild the area with plastic wood. Give piece its final shape by sanding with progressively finer grades of sandpaper. Carve details indicated by fine lines on patterns, and sand gently; use an emery board for hard-to-reach areas. Paint piece, letting each color dry before painting adjacent areas. For a primitive look, no blending or shading is used on these pieces. Apply large areas of flat color first, and work progressively to smallest details. See photos and individual directions.

**Watermelon and Slice:** Start with a block of wood 9″ × 9″ × 13″. Use a lathe to cut a cylinder 8″ in diameter. Use knives and rasps to roughly round the ends, shaping the stump of a stem at one end, and referring to photo. Using coping saw, cut out one wedge. Sand only lightly, so wedge fits neatly back in place. With wedge in place, paint outside of watermelon: Paint light green with 10 stripes of medium and dark green from center of one end to center of other end. Mottle stripes by pressing brush flatly in various directions all over stripes. Use fine liner brush to paint irregular veinings all over surface. Paint stem and center of opposite end brown. Remove wedge. Paint both wedge and cut-out section of big piece as follows: Paint within ⅛″ of edges light green. Paint a ⅜″ stripe beside it pale green, then a ¼″ stripe of off-white. Paint rest of area a rosy red. Let dry, then paint on teardrop-shaped seeds with black.

59

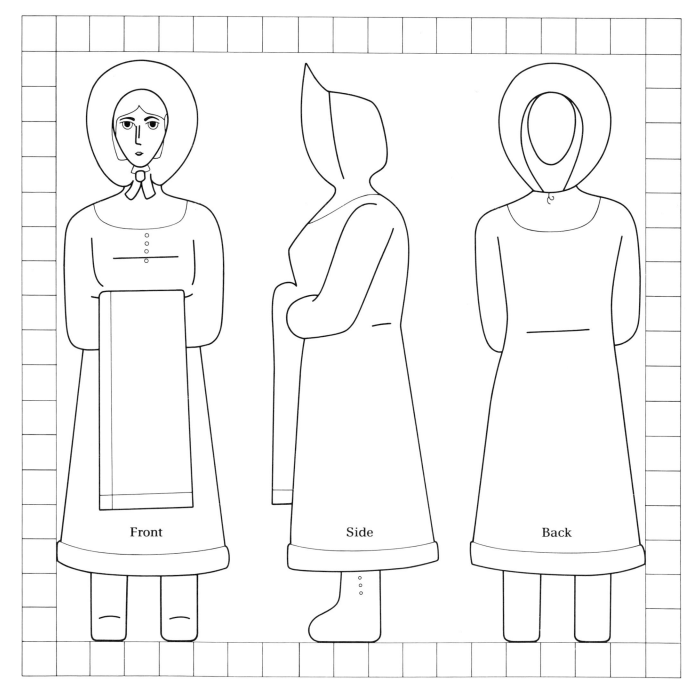

Front      Side      Back

**PATTERNS FOR QUILT LADY**    Each square = 1″

Front　　　　　　　Side　　　　　　　Back

PATTERNS FOR CIGAR STORE INDIAN　　Each square = 1″

**Quilt Lady:** Begin with a block of wood 5″ × 6″ × 18″. Strive for smooth, round body. Make back of bonnet almost flat, and gouge out front of brim, setting it back from the face ¼″. Except for brows and nose, keep face fairly flat. Quilt is flat and square, except for rounded top edge.

*Base:* From 2″-thick wood, cut a 3½″ × 4½″ rectangle. Bevel edges at a 45 degree angle along one large (top) surface, until it measures 2½″ × 3½″. Stand figure on this surface, centering carefully. Trace around each foot. Measuring carefully, drill a hole at center of each foot and each foot tracing on base. Glue a prong into each hole on base.

*Painting:* Paint base and dress taupe, collar white, and boots black. Paint quilt white. Except for a square at lower left corner, paint borders on left side and bottom edge pink. Paint bonnet blue, hair brown. Using liner brush, paint eyebrows, eyes, and mouth; leave rest of face unpainted. With gold paint, dot 4 buttons below collar at center front of dress, and 3 buttons at top side of each boot. Trace actual-size stencil pattern for quilt (page 64). Transfer to clear adhesive and cut out with Xacto knife. Adhere to front of quilt ⅛″ from bottom border and centered across white area. With a nearly dry brush, pounce brown paint over cutout of basket and handle, pink over cutouts of flowers, green over cutouts of stems. Let dry, then lift stencil and repeat twice above, ⅛″ apart.

**Cigar Store Indian:** Begin with a block of wood 7″ × 8″ × 25″. Side shown is right side; allow extra leeway for slightly higher raise of hand, and tomahawk on left side. Use large chisel blades to undercut forearms, to shape skirt, for folds in cape, and for feathers in headdress. Use small chisel blades for hair, knuckles, small feathers on clothing, cigars, fur on tops of shoes. Use point of knife to stipple headdress, carve small rectangular bars at base of each feather, make an angular face with deep wrinkles around mouth. Dig out between tomahawk handle and shirt front.

*Painting:* Work from the top down. Paint headdress feathers white, with black tips. Paint red below feathers, with a rectangular bar, striped in yellow, aqua, blue, and brown, at the base of each feather. Paint stippled band of headdress gray. Paint hair black, hair wrappings white. Paint whites of eyes, black pupils and eyebrows; paint lips and wrinkles mauve; leave rest of face and hands unpainted. Paint scarf at neck in turquoise, with dabs of light aqua and taupe. Paint shirt and pants tan, with deeper shades for edgings. Paint armbands red; add a white diamond at center of each. Paint skirt red, cape and belt blue. Paint between legs, and between legs and cape white. Paint small feathers as follows: innermost areas turquoise on skirt, multicolored on side of cape; center areas white; outer areas black. Paint tomahawk handle and cigars dark brown, with a light brown wrapper around center of cigars. Paint tomahawk and knife blades gray, knife handle white. Paint tops of shoes taupe, sides dark brown.

63

ACTUAL-SIZE  STENCIL PATTERN
FOR QUILT LADY

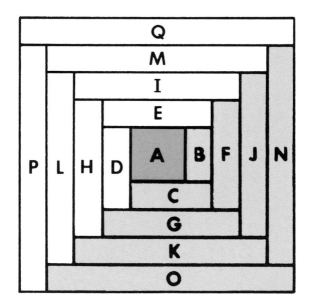

DIAGRAM FOR LOG CABIN QUILT BLOCK
A = darkest tone

# Log Cabin Quilt

*Size:* Approximately 90″ square.

*Materials:* Cotton fabrics 44″-45″ wide: red print (includes backing), 6 yds.; various dark prints (shades of taupe, blue, green, and red), 3 yds. total; various light prints (white, beige, pink, peach), 3 yds. total. Quilt batting. Ecru sewing thread. Red and white quilting thread. (See photo page 63.)

*Directions:* Read "General Directions for Quilting," page 152. Quilt is composed of a pattern of 36 quilt blocks, each with a red square in the center, and each divided diagonally in half with light-colored patches on one side, dark-colored patches on the other. First, cut from red fabric one 92″ length across full width, and two 26″ × 92″ rectangles; set aside for backing.

*Patches:* Refer to Diagram for Log Cabin Quilt Block. A = 3½″ square; all other patches are 2″ wide, lengths as indicated: B—3½″, C and D—5″, E and F—6½″, G and H—8″, I and J—9½″, K and L—11″, M and N—12½″, O and P—14″, Q—15½″.

Avoid confusion: when cutting patches, make piles of each size patch, string each pile together with needle and thread, then remove needle and lift off patches as needed for patchwork. From solid red, cut 36 A. From dark-colored fabrics, cut 36 of each of the following patches, cutting the following pairs from the same fabric: B and C, F and G, J and K, N and O. Vary the fabrics; for example, for patch B, you may wish to cut 10 each from taupe calico, 8 from dark green print, 10 from a blue gray fabric, and 8 from brown. Next cut 36 of the following patches from light-colored fabrics, cutting the following

pairs from the same fabric: D and E, H and I, L and M, P and Q.

*Quilt Block:* Make 36. Stitch patches together right sides facing and making ¼″ seams. Apply patches in alphabetical order, working in rounds. Press seams flat. Finished quilt blocks should measure approximately 15½″ square, including seam allowance all around.

*Quilt Top Assembly:* Arrange quilt blocks in six rows of six. Referring to photograph, rotate each block so light-colored patches are on top or on bottom, as shown. Overall pattern of quilt top should feature dark-colored, then light-colored diamonds. Stitch quilt blocks together in each row, matching seams, then stitch rows together.

*Assembly:* Piece quilt backing: Stitch a 26″ × 92″ rectangle to either side of larger piece. Center quilt top over backing, right sides facing, then place both, centered, over batting. Smooth and pin. Stitch all around quilt top, ¼″ from edges, leaving an opening along one side for turning. Clip corners, trim batting close to seam and backing ½″ from seam. Turn quilt to right side and slip-stitch opening closed. Smooth again and pin with safety pins to keep layers from shifting.

*To Tuft:* Thread needle with double strand of candlewicking cotton. Insert needle in center of each red A patch, through all layers, then bring needle back to quilt top, ⅛″ away. Tie ends in a square knot and clip ends ¼″ from knot.

*To Quilt:* Start from the center of quilt and quilt outwards in all directions; use quilting thread. In each quilt block, stitch around each round of patches, ⅛″ inside seams. Referring to Diagram for Quilt Block, quilt around patch A, then around B, C, D, and E patches, then around F, G, H, and I patches, and so on.

65

# The Living Room

GOTHIC CHURCH
PUTZ VILLAGE
CROCHETED TABLE RUNNER
PINEAPPLE ANTIQUE HOOKED RUG
REVERSE PAINTING ON GLASS
LADY LIBERTY AND UNCLE SAM
APPLIQUÉD PILLOWS
HEART QUILT FOR DOLL

he charm of this well-used country living room lies in its simplicity. The soft curves of the stout 1930s couch, chair, and ottoman counterbalance the linear lines of the room; rosy cinnamon-colored upholstery fabric communicates warmth, as do the hand-hewn beams of the ceiling and the nutmeg stain of the wide-plank floors of this restored Vermont farmhouse. Lending subtle elegance are Victorian lace curtains and the narrow oak shelf, which is probably an early American wooden valence cut down.

The majestic architectural model of a Gothic church is a copy of an antique I saw illustrated in a magazine. Small hinges are attached to the roof section allowing one to raise the roof and use the inside of the box for storage. It thus becomes a handy "catch all" for bric-a-brac and keepsakes for which no other place can be found. Architectural models were made in a great variety of styles and shapes, and today are prized by collectors. For a more extravagant display, a miniature putz village has been placed around the Gothic church, along with antique brass candlesticks (page 71). Putz villages of little wooden houses and churches traditionally were made by the Pennsylvania Germans and placed under the tree at Christmastime. As new structures were added over the years, the village evolved into a nostalgic reminder of holidays past and eventually became a family heirloom.

The coffee table in the living room is actually a kitchen table with cut-down legs. Placed over the tabletop is a crocheted table runner made by my husband's grandmother. This handmade treasure was preserved over the years in a trunk until it was kindly given to me.

Although the early history and origin of the crochet technique is difficult to trace, it is believed that this handcraft was derived from the decorative lace traditions of the 13th century. Crochet developed as a cottage industry in Ireland after the famine, and the exquisitely beautiful and technically challenging patterns of Victorian crochet are well known. When the needlework technique came to America in the 19th century, it enjoyed wide acceptance as evidenced by the doilies, bedspreads, and ornamented linen and clothing found in some measure in every American home even today. Using a simple hook, crochet consists of making a succession of loops in a continuous thread; a simple chain or a series of chains form the basis of most patterns.

On the floor is Pineapple Antique, a hooked rug by Marion N. Ham (page 74). It displays a romantic overall design recalling expensive imported English carpets. This rug shows a center pineapple motif, symbolizing hospitality, entwined with leaves, stylized flowers, and vines against a black field. (Many antique hooked rugs no longer have strong black areas as in this rug because the black dye over time has faded to a muddy green.) A floral vine border unites the design and gives the rug an integrated feeling.

In a more formal living room is an antique mirror with a rare example of "reverse painting on glass," a homely art of the 18th and 19th centuries (page 78). Young women created these works of art to give as gifts or to decorate their own walls at home. Due to the highly fragile nature of the glass, few good examples remain intact. "Reverse painting on glass" is a technique in which the chosen image is painted on the reverse side of the glass with translucent paints; when dry, the image is turned over and framed. When the image is backed with tinsel, the composition takes on a metallic appearance. Depicted frequently were fruit and flower still lifes and sometimes scenes of homesteads and churches. The lovely church in this "reverse painting on glass" is executed in bright yellow, creating a brilliant contrast with the blue sky and the green trees. Tiny pinpricks add outline to the structures and give detail to the trees.

Patriotism has remained a favorite theme of folk artists. Throughout history America has experienced great periods of patriotism—at the time of the American Revolution, after the death of beloved leader George Washington, and during the Centennial celebration of our Independence. Responding to the same spirit, Americans across the United States recently stitched, carved, and painted patriotic folk art in honor of the Centennial celebration of the Statue of Liberty. The two appliquéd pillows were designed in a neo-naive style. Lady Liberty shelters two immigrant children, while holding an American flag; Uncle Sam extends a French tri-couleur to an unseen citizen. Combining embroidered stencil-shaped letters spelling "LIBERTY" and "JUSTICE," with hand-lettered sentiments inspired by national anthems, these two pillows become historical statements in and of themselves (page 79).

On the wall hangs my appliquéd heart quilt (page 2). It is a traditional doll's quilt made of scraps of fabric: cuttings from garments long outgrown or too threadbare to patch—an infant's dress, grandmother's apron, a husband's homespun shirt. These precious keepsake quilts become family mementos of great sentimental value. Looking at an old quilt is looking at history. I recall the days when I stitched this particular sweet remembrance; I inscribed "remember me" on every block. I made three of these doll's quilts, one for each of my children. They all hang in frames and will be presented to the children when they start homes of their own.

Hanging next to the quilt is The Chase Sampler. It is a remarkably designed sampler, now available as a reproduction kit from the Colonial Williamsburg restoration in Williamsburg, Virginia.

# Gothic Church

*Size:* 16½" high.

*Materials:* Sheet of masonite, 2' × 4'. Small scrap of wood, for chimney. Four 1" finials, available from lumber or dollhouse miniature store. Spackling compound. Latex high gloss enamel paint: brick red, black, white. Finishing nails, ¾". Wood glue.

*Equipment:* Pencil. Paper. L- or T-square. Masking tape. Black permanent ink felt-tip marker. Coping saw or band saw. Hammer. Flat paintbrushes, 1" and ³⁄₁₆" widths.

*Directions:* Following schematic diagrams, measure and mark patterns on sheets of paper. Use L- or T-square to ensure right angles; draw arched and round windows in placements shown. Cut out patterns, making duplicates as needed so you have a pattern for each piece: For main structure (MS), cut 1 each Front and Back, 2 Sides, 2 Rooves. For Apses (A), cut 1 each Front and Back, 4 Sides, 4 Rooves, cutting out corner shown for 2 of the rooves. For Front Entry (FE), cut 1 Front (with door), 2 Sides, 1 Roof. For Spire (S), cut 1 Front, 2 Sides, 1 Back, 1 Roof.

Lay pattern pieces out on masonite, with edges parallel to sides of masonite. For rooves on A Front and Back, reverse pattern to cut second and fourth roof. Tape patterns in place and trace around them with felt-tip marker. Use saw to cut out. Remove patterns, and set aside for further use.

To assemble pieces, apply wood glue to adjacent sides, fit together, and use masking tape to hold. Then nail through edges ½" from corners to secure. Fit walls together at right angles, so that cut edges of first piece mentioned butt and are concealed by wrong side of second piece. First, assemble main structure: Make a four-sided box by placing MS Sides at either short end of MS Front and Back, matching 6" sides. Fit MS Rooves on top, then remove and bevel edges with sanding block to come together in a point; roof will overhang Front and Back slightly and extend past Sides. Glue and nail roof in place. Cut notch a small scrap block of wood as indicated for chimney; carve a scrap of wood for chimney top and glue in place. Glue chimney over roof, ½" from left side. For apses, join A Front and Back each with Sides, then place an apse, centered, over MS Front and Back. Bevel edges of A Rooves same as for MS Rooves, and glue on top, gluing sloped side to MS Rooves and cut-out section of 2 roof pieces coming together over front apse. Join FE Sides to front entry. Center front entry on front apse, all bottom edges flush with table-top surface. For spire, glue S Sides and S Back to top of S Front, glue spire roof on top, then insert all the way into cut-out in front entry roof; glue generously around roof cut-out to secure spire.

Use spackling compound to fill in any areas where pieces don't meet exactly. Let dry. Using wide brush, paint all rooves except spire roof black; paint walls and entire spire brick red; paint chimney white. Let dry. Cut out arched and round windows and door on marked patterns. Lay patterns over corresponding walls and spire front. Trace around cutouts to mark position of windows and door with pencil. Paint black within outlines; let dry, then outline in white, using narrower paintbrush, and using a straight-edge to keep lines straight and clean at sides and across sills. Paint finials white and glue to top of spire roof.

# SCHEMATIC DRAWINGS
## FOR GOTHIC CHURCH

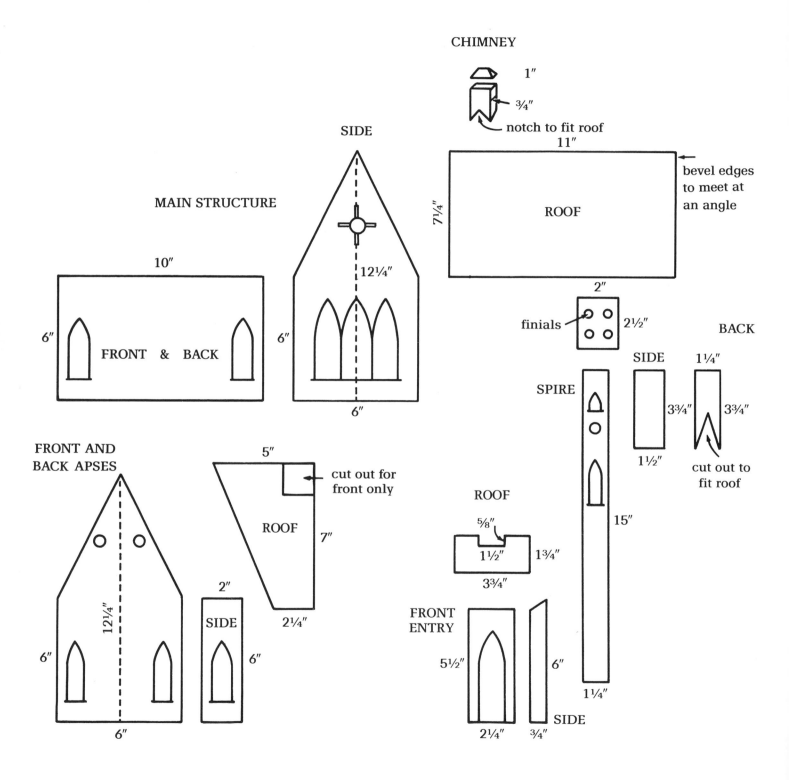

CHIMNEY

1″

¾″

notch to fit roof

11″

7¼″

ROOF

bevel edges
to meet at
an angle

SIDE

12¼″

MAIN STRUCTURE

10″

6″

FRONT & BACK

6″

6″

2″

finials

2½″

SIDE

1½″

3¾″

BACK

1¼″

3¾″

cut out to
fit roof

SPIRE

15″

1¼″

ROOF

⅝″

1½″

1¾″

3¾″

5″

cut out for
front only

ROOF

7″

2¼″

FRONT AND
BACK APSES

12¼″

6″

6″

2″

SIDE

6″

6″

FRONT
ENTRY

5½″

6″

SIDE

2¼″

¾″

72

ACTUAL-SIZE
SCHEMATIC DIAGRAMS
FOR PUTZ VILLAGE

HOUSE

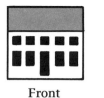

Front        Side

CHURCH

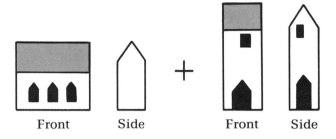

Front    Side    +    Front    Side

## *Putz Village*

**Sizes:** House, ¾″ high; church, 1⅛″ high.

**Materials:** Scraps of softwood ¼″ thick. Acrylic paint: aqua, purple, tan, black, blue. Wood glue. Varnish (optional).

**Equipment:** Coping saw. Penknife. Sandpaper. Fine paintbrushes.

**Directions:** Schematic diagrams are shown actual-size. Cut a piece of wood to same size and shape as each Front piece, using coping saw. Turn piece on its side, and mark angle of roof as shown in Side diagrams with pencil. Mark same angle along opposite side. Using penknife, cut across top surface of wood pieces, carving away until shape of each side simulates corresponding diagram. Sand all pieces smooth.

*Finishing:* For house, paint walls aqua, paint roof on front and back surfaces tan. When dry, paint door and windows on front only, referring to diagram but painting freehand. For church, paint rooves on front and back surfaces blue. Paint doors and windows black. Leave walls unpainted. Glue main structure and bell tower together, with bottom edges even. If desired, give miniatures two thin coats of varnish.

# Crocheted Table Runner

**Sizes:** Small—14″w × 24″l,  Large—13″w × 35″l.

**Materials:** *Small Runner:* Size 20 crochet thread, 2 balls. Steel crochet hook size 8. *Large Runner:* Size 30 crochet thread, 2 balls. Steel crochet hook size 9.

**Gauge:** 14 dc = 1″; 5 rows = 1″ on 8 hook and Size 20 thread. 15 dc = 1″; 6 rows = 1″ on 9 hook and Size 30 thread.

**Directions:** *Note:* Variations in size and length are achieved by different size hooks, threads and number of pat row repeats. With size hook and thread given for size runner desired, ch 219. **Row 1:** Work 2 dc in 3rd ch from hook, *(ch 5, sk 5 ch, sc in next ch) 3 times, ch 5, sk 5 ch, 3 dc in next ch; rep from *, end 3 dc in last ch. Ch 3, turn. **Row 2:** Sk next dc, dc in next dc, 2 dc in next ch 5 lp, *(ch 5, sk next sc, sc in next ch 5 lp) twice, ch 5, sk next sc, 3 dc in next ch 5 lp, ch 2, sk next 3 dc, 3 dc in next ch 5 lp; rep from *, end 2 dc in last ch 5 lp, dc in next dc, sk next dc, dc in top of turning ch, Ch 3, turn. **Row 3:** *Dc in next 3 dc, 3 dc in next ch 5 lp, ch 5, sk next sc, sc in next ch 5 lp, ch 5, sk next sc, 3 dc in next ch 5 lp, dc in next 3 dc, ch 2; rep from *, end 3 dc in last ch 5 lp, dc in next 3 dc, dc in top of turning ch. Ch 3, turn. **Row 4:** *Dc in next 6 dc, 3 dc in next ch 5 lp, ch 4, 3 dc in next ch 5 lp, dc in next 6 dc, ch 2; rep from *, end dc in last 6 dc, dc in top of turning ch. Ch 3, turn. **Row 5:** * Dc in next 6 dc, ch 5, sk next 3 dc, sc in next ch 4 lp, ch 5, sk next 3 dc, dc in next 6 dc, ch 2; rep from *, end ch 5, sk next 3 dc, dc in last 6 dc, dc in top of turning ch. Ch 3, turn. **Row 6:** * Dc in next 3 dc, sk next 3 dc, (ch 5, sc in next ch 5 lp) twice, ch 5, sk next 3 dc, dc in next 3 dc, ch 2; rep from *, end ch 5, sk next 3 dc, dc in last 3 dc, dc in top of turning ch. Ch 3, turn. **Row 7:** Work 2 dc in first dc, * (ch 5, sc in next ch 5 lp) 3 times, ch 5, sk next 3 dc, dc in next ch 2 sp; rep from *, end ch 5, sk next 2 dc, 2 dc in last dc, dc in turning ch. Ch 3, turn. Rep Rows 2–7 for pat 15 times more for small and 33 times more for large runner. At end of last row ch 1, turn.

*Edging:* **Rnd 1:** Sl st to first ch 5 lp, ch 3, in same lp work 1 dc and ch 2 and 2 dc beg shell made; (ch 5, sc in next ch 5 lp) 3 times, ch 5, * in center dc of next 3 dc work 2 dc and ch 2 and 2 dc — shell made, (ch 5, sc in next ch 5 lp) 4 times, ch 5; rep from * to next corner, end with (ch 5, sc in next ch 5 lp) 3 times, ch 5, shell in last ch 5 lp, ch 5, shell in sp formed by turning ch at end of row, working along next edge ** ch 5, shell in end of next row, (ch 5, sc in next ch 5 lp) 4 times; rep from ** to end of second row before next corner, end with ch 5, shell in end of next row, ch 5, shell in end of last row, ch 5, shell in next ch lp along edge of same last row; continue in this way around remaining 2 edges, end shell in end of last row, ch 4, join to top of ch 3 at beg. **Rnd 2:** Sl st to ch 2 sp of first shell, beg shell in same sp, (ch 5, sk next sc, sc in next ch 5 lp) twice, * ch 5, shell in ch 2 sp of next shell—shell over shell made; (ch 5, sk next sc, sc in next ch 5 lp) 3 times; rep from * to next corner, end with (ch 5, sk next sc, sc in next ch 5 lp) twice, ch 5, (shell over shell, ch 5) 3 times; continue this way around, end ch 5, join to beg shell. **Rnd 3:** Sl st to ch 2 sp, beg shell, ch 6, sk next sc, sc in next ch 5 lp, ch 6, shell over shell, ch 6, sk next sc, sc in next ch 5 lp, ch 5, sc in next ch 5 lp, ch 6, shell over shell and continue around working ch 6 between corner shells, join. **Rnd 4:** Sl st to ch 2 sp of first shell, beg shell, ch 9, sc in sc, ch 9, shell over shell, ch 9, sk next sc, sc in next ch lp, ch 9, shell over shell and continue around working ch 9 between corner shells, join. Fasten off.

PATTERN FOR PINEAPPLE ANTIQUE HOOKED RUG    Each square = 1″

ACTUAL-SIZE PATTERN FOR REVERSE PAINTING ON GLASS

## Pineapple Antique Hooked Rug

**Size:** 36″ × 70½″.

Read "General Directions for Hooked Rugs" on page 153. Enlarge pattern on paper ruled into 1″ squares. For pineapples, work diamond shapes in rose on a yellow-gray tweed background; outline leaves in gray and fill in with olive green. Flowers throughout rug combine different values and textures of rose, yellow, or gray and yellow. For leaves of the flowers, use sage green. Vines are 1 row taupe and 1 row red tweed. Background and outer edge of rug are brown. Border stems and leaves are in a green/black plaid. Use solid, uneven tones of tan for the background.

## Reverse Painting on Glass

**Size:** Design area, 6½″ × 4″.

**Materials:** Sheet of glass, approximately 6½″ × 4″: Use picture glass, then place in its frame, or, if desired, use a mirror with a design area at the top. Mirror shown is a one-of-a-kind antique; however, a sleeker, simpler walnut framed mirror with space at the top for art is available to order. (For Petite Mirror in Walnut, #20071, with design area 7″ × 5″, write Sudberry House, Box 895, Old Lyme, CT 06371.) Acrylic paints. Small paintbrushes, fine, tapered liner and flat, and one straight pin.

**Directions:** Trace actual-size design onto tracing paper. Turn to reverse side, and go over any lines that are difficult to see. Center this reverse of design under glass; tape to secure.

To paint on glass, you will be working from the back of the picture; what you paint will be seen in reverse. Start with the smallest details first, and progress to the main elements and finally to the large areas of color in background and foreground. Unless otherwise indicated, let each element dry before you add another behind it. Blend colors on a palette, and strive for muted shades.

First, using a fine, tapered brush, paint all the details of the church in slate gray: doors, windows, steps, lines of spire and cross, dots and finials around roof. Using a flat brush, paint the roof a dark shrimp color. Paint the walls of the church a greenish yellow, stroking color over windows and door; paint fence in same color. Paint tree trunks light brown; dip a straight pin into the black paint and prick color as indicated in diagram; dab light and dark green and blue-green all over treetops. Paint sidewalk across center of picture in shades of peach and mustard. When these main elements are thoroughly dry, paint foreground gray-green. Let dry, then paint sky: Stroke a rosy shade of pink behind church, painting across entire width of glass to within ½″ of treetops. Before this area of color is dry, paint upper portion of sky blue, stroking across full width of picture and blending into rosy sky section.

Let all paint dry; turn to right side and frame. (See page 78.)

ACTUAL-SIZE PATTERN
FOR LADY LIBERTY PILLOW

OF THEE I SING

MY · COUNTRY
TIS · OF · THEE
SWEET·LAND
-OF-
LIBERTY

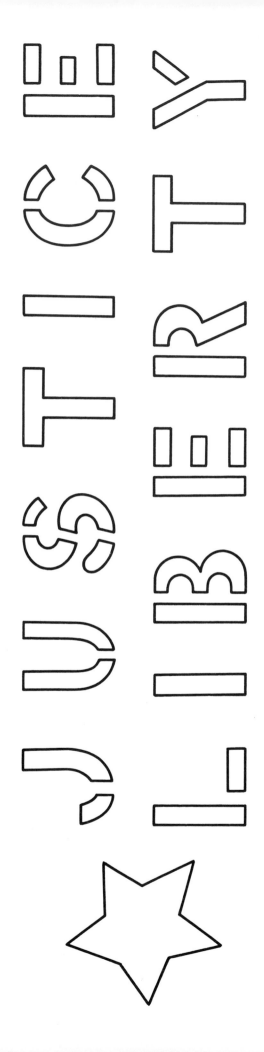

## Lady Liberty and Uncle Sam Appliquéd Pillows

**Size:** Both, 13¼″ × 15½″.

**Materials:** Preshrunk cotton fabrics 44″–45″ wide: Unbleached muslin ⅜ yd.; royal blue calico, ⅛ yd.; scraps of bleached muslin, flesh tone, blue-gray, red, black, and other colors as listed below. Thread to match fabrics. Brown permanent ink felt-tip pen. Polyester fiberfill.

*For Lady Liberty Pillow:* Fabric scraps in gray-green, light blue, gold, pale yellow, and blue with white polka dots. Six-strand embroidery floss: 1 skein royal blue, small amount of taupe.

*For Uncle Sam Pillow:* Navy fabric scraps. Six strand embroidery floss: 1 skein red, small amount brown.

**Directions:** *For each pillow:* From unbleached muslin, cut two 14¼″ × 16½″ rectangles, with straight edges along grain of fabric. Trace patterns for pillow onto tracing paper. Heavy lines indicate appliqué outlines; fine lines indicate lettering to be inked or details to be embroidered. Center pictorial pattern horizontally across one muslin rectangle. Insert dressmaker's carbon ink side down in between and go over all lines with sharp pencil, to transfer. In same manner, transfer word LIBERTY or JUSTICE 1″ from top edge and centered between side edges. Go over fine lettering (phrases) with brown felt-tip pen. For appliqué pieces, place patterns on fabrics as indicated below, keeping patterns ½″ from fabric edges and ½″ apart. Use dressmaker's carbon to transfer as before. Cut out pieces ¼″ beyond marked lines, for seam allowance.

Working in the order numbered in

FREEDOM
-AND-
JUSTICE
FOR·ALL

OUR COUNTRY
OUR DESTINY

ACTUAL-SIZE PATTERN FOR UNCLE SAM PILLOW

individual directions, pin appliqués to their corresponding shape on background. Working in the same order, turn edges not overlapped by another piece under ¼" and slip-stitch each piece in place with tiny stitches in matching thread. Add embroidery as indicated, referring to "Embroidery Stitch Details" on page 151.

*Lady Liberty Pillow:* From pale yellow fabric, cut outer flames of torch (1). From gold, cut inner flame of torch (2). From gray-green fabric, cut handle of torch (3), Liberty's crown (8), and gown (9). From flesh tone fabric, cut her arm and hands (4), face (5) and faces of the children (11). From gray, cut her hair (6) and shoe (7). From blue-gray, cut boy's suit (9) and hat (12). From blue, cut girl's dress (10). From black, cut girl's hair (13) and the children's shoes (14). From bleached muslin, cut the entire flag shape (15). From red, cut stripes on flag (16), and 4 stars, for corners of the pillow. From blue dot, cut "stars" portion of flag (17).

*Embroidery:* Using 3 strands of taupe floss, chain-stitch flagpole, and make a French knot for all eyes. Using two strands of taupe, straight-stitch all other facial features. Using three strands of blue floss, satin-stitch the word LIBERTY with vertical stitches.

*Uncle Sam Pillow:* From red, cut hat crown (1), pants stripes (8), red flag panel (11), and 4 stars for sides of pillow. From bleached muslin, cut white hat stripes (2), hair (4), pants (7), white flag panel (12). From flesh tone, cut face (3), hand (6). From blue-gray, cut hat brim (5), jacket (9), blue flag panel (13). From black, cut shoes (10).

*Embroidery:* Using 3 strands of brown floss, chain-stitch the flagpole, and make a French knot eye. Using 1 strand of brown floss, straight-stitch the mouth. Using 3 strands of red floss, satin-stitch the word JUSTICE with vertical stitches. Use one strand of blue sewing thread to stem-stitch the furl of the flag on the red panel.

*Border Strips:* From royal blue calico, cut strips along the grain ⅞" wide and the following lengths: two 11", two 9¼", two 14¼" and two 16". Turn long edges ¼" to wrong side and press. Pin 11" strips horizontally across pillow front, 3" from top and bottom edges and centered between sides. Pin 9¼" strips vertically 3" from sides, with ends turned under ¼" and overlapping horizontal strips. Slip-stitch along all edges using tiny stitches and blue thread. Pin 16" strips across pillow ¼" outside 11" strips, then place 14¼" strips to the outside of 9¼" strips; stitch in place as before.

*Stars:* Turn edges under and slip-stitch in place, along sides on Uncle Sam Pillow, at corners on Lady Liberty Pillow.

*Assembly:* Place fabric rectangles together, right sides facing. Stitch all around, ½" from edges, leaving 4" along center of bottom edge unstitched. Clip corners, turn to right side. Stuff pillow plumply, and slip-stitch opening closed.

Remember Me

ACTUAL-SIZE
APPLIQUÉ PATTERN FOR HEART QUILT

How to Appliqué

# Heart Quilt for Doll

**Size:** 22¼" × 26½".

**Materials:** Cotton fabrics 44"–45" wide: unbleached muslin, 1½ yds.; tan pin-dot print, ¼ yd.; maroon pin-dot, ⅛ yd.; scraps of 12 other assorted small prints and baby ginghams. Sewing thread to match. Fine, brown permanent ink felt-tip pen.

**Directions:** Read "General Directions for Quilting" on page 152.

*Note:* This quilt does not have batting between the quilt top and backing, although you may add it if you so wish. From muslin, cut a 23¼" × 27½" rectangle; set aside for backing. From remaining muslin, cut out 30 rectangles, 4" × 4⅛", for quilt blocks.

*Appliqués:* Make a template for actual-size heart pattern. Use to cut out 30 heart appliqués from assorted colored fabrics. Clip into seam allowances along curves and across bottom corner. Turn seam allowances to wrong side and press.

*Quilt Block:* (Make 30.) Pin a heart to each muslin rectangle, ⅞" from one 4" edge (top) and centered between side edges. Slip-stitch in place with tiny stitches all around. Trace actual-size pattern for heart and Remember Me script. Pin over each heart, insert dressmaker's carbon paper and transfer lettering. Remove pattern and carbon and go over lettering with fine felt-tip pen.

*Assembly:* Lay out quilt blocks in a pleasing arrangement of 6 horizontal rows of 5 blocks each. Stitch blocks together in each row, then stitch rows together. Quilt top should measure 18" × 22⅛", including seam allowance all around.

*Borders:* For inner border, cut strips from maroon pin-dot fabric: two

1⅛″ × 22⅛″, two 1⅛″ × 19¼″. Stitch longer strips to sides of quilt top, then stitch shorter strips to top and bottom. For outer border, cut strips from tan pin-dot fabric: two 2¼″ × 23⅜″ and two 2¼″ × 22¾″. Stitch to quilt top same as for inner borders. Place quilt top on backing with right sides facing, and stitch all around, ¼″ from outside edges of borders; leave 6″ along center of bottom edge unstitched. Trim backing to match quilt top, clip corners, and turn quilt to right side. Slip-stitch opening closed.

*Quilting:* Pin layers to keep them from shifting. Working from the center outward, quilt around each heart, first ⅛″ from appliqué edges, then again, ⅛″ beyond first quilting line. Quilt all around joined quilt blocks, ⅛″ inside inner border. Quilt all around inner border, ⅛″ inside outer border.

# The Master Bedroom

A four-poster, canopied bed fills a snug corner of this cozy country bedroom. One might feel a reluctance to disturb the elegance created by these "fancy" handcrafts; however, my pink-and-white geometric quilt, in a pattern called Trip Around the World, is made of a practical, sturdy cotton. Historically, this pattern is one of the earliest, most common, and simplest to work. A variation of the One Patch, it requires that single patches of fabric prints, calicoes, and solids be cut and pieced together to form concentric squares radiating from the center of the quilt. Because the pattern calls for making one patch at a time, the homemaker of early America could gather and use every scrap for this fabric-efficient quilt. Most households saved every remnant of cloth for quilt making. Quilters relied on the indigo barrel, which characteristically stood in the kitchen, and on linsey woolsey, the stiff-textured and limited-color cloth that was a household staple. Quilters grew to love the crisp, clean look of white and indigo and created coverlets of every pattern variation one could conjure.

Crochet can bring a wonderful elegance to linens. Based on the one chain stitch, a vast variety of designs developed over the years and crocheted edging became a widespread folk-craft expression. Using white cotton or silk thread, the crocheter would embellish towels, pillowcases, bedcovers, and bedclothes. Linda Allen designed and crocheted the intricately scalloped pillowcase edging depicting the most popular folk-art motif of all time—the heart. The pretty and romantic pillowcase is seen on the living-room couch with another craft by Linda—a quilt remnant pillow made from a portable quilt block (page 90). Linda was inspired by the Star of Bethlehem pattern. A combination of tan, navy, pink, and white, this pattern demands precision and skill. For neatness and accuracy, particularly in pieced quilts containing long and slender points, small patches used to be basted to a paper lining, with a narrow margin of cloth folded over the paper. Then, with two edges held together, the seam was whipped with tiny over-and-over stitches. No portion of a quilt was considered obscure enough to allow for a less-than-perfect stitch.

Another folk craft that demands patience and competence is called fraktur. In the early 1700s Protestant German-speaking people brought the tradition of illustrated birth *(Geburts)*, baptismal *(Taufschein)*, and wedding *(Trau)* certificates to our shores. The art is derived from illuminated texts of medieval times. Highly decorative watercolor renderings of the tulip, dove, and heart combined with stylized Gothic lettering is characteristic of fraktur. Usually executed by schoolmasters and the clergy, fraktur flourished until the 19th century when printed certificates with fill-in spaces brought on the decline of the hand-painted versions.

Painting in the fraktur tradition, Linda has recorded the family lineage of her great-grandmother in ink and watercolor on paper. She gave the work a religious tone by adding Biblical references. Her fanciful ornamentation and plain script create a highly personal, artistic expression (page 94).

The Songbird hooked rug is a sentimental work of birds and flowers. It was hooked by Bessie Ricker and designed by Marion N. Ham, both of Maine. Placed on a blue-painted floor, it adds warmth and charm to the bedroom (page 97). Folded over a red-painted blanket chest from 19th-century New England is an antique geometric quilt called Hovering Hawks. It is pieced predominantly in brown, coral, and white triangles, and although at close inspection the pattern appears to be a random arrangement of triangles, from a distance one can discern a concentric band of color surrounding a center square. It can be seen in full on the side of a barn on page 163.

In front of the bathroom in the master bedroom is my painted floorcloth (page 150). Using stencils or by painting freehand, resourceful folk artists would copy designs from expensive and rare rugs onto a canvas-like material. Interweaving vines in subtle greens, stylized flowers, and bluebirds are an unusual Victorian-like design for this unpretentious craft material.

A turned-spindle hall table painted black is dressed in an antique tea cloth with a simple repeating design done in crochet. Linda's handmade band box holds embroidery thread. Although this box is lined with a newspaper from the 19th century, it was not uncommon to line band boxes with hand-painted fraktur. These delightful boxes were used for keeping small trinkets.

# Trip Around the World Quilt

*Size:* 70" square.

*Materials:* Cotton fabrics, 44" wide: White for backing, 4 yds.; one pink print for border, 2 yds.; a second pink print for binding, ½ yd.; smaller amounts of up to 22 other pink prints. White sewing and quilting thread. Quilt batting.

*Directions:* Read "General Directions for Quilting" on page 152. From largest quantity of print fabric, cut borders: two strips 3½" × 66" and two 3½" × 71". From another print, cut 1¾"-wide strips across full width of fabric; piece until strip measures 8 yards in length and set aside for quilt binding.

*Patches:* With graph paper, make template for a 2" square. Use template to cut patches, using same print to cut an entire round. Vary shades of fabric from one round to the next, striving for light and dark contrasts. For round 1, cut 1 square. For round 2, cut 4 squares. For round 3, cut 8 squares. Continue in this manner, cutting 4 more square patches for each succeeding round than the previous round, until you reach round 24, with 92 squares.

*Quilt Top:* Following pattern established in assembly diagram, lay out square patches on a large flat surface. Begin in the center with round 1. At each edge of this square, place a square of round 2. At each outside edge of round 2 squares, place a round 3 square. Surround round 3 with round 4. Continue in this pattern until all rounds are in place. Stitch square patches together into horizontal rows, then stitch rows together, taking care to match seams. Cut diagonally along squares of round 24 to straighten sides of quilt top; see dash lines in trimming diagram. Stitch shorter border strips at opposite sides of quilt top, then stitch longer strips across top and bottom of quilt, continuing sewing across ends of side borders.

*Assembly:* Piece backing: cut white fabric into two 72" lengths across full width of fabric; cut one lengthwise in half and sew each half to sides of whole piece. Trim dimensions to ½" larger all around than quilt top.

*Layer Quilt:* Place backing wrong side down on a flat surface, with batting and quilt top, right side up, on top. Baste layers to secure.

*To Quilt:* Start from the center and work outwards in all directions. Choose either of 3 methods: 1) Stitch along all seams between square patches. 2) Stitch around each round of patches, working diagonally along the center of each patch in round. 3) Quilt as in method 2, but work only around every other round.

*Binding:* Trim backing and batting even with quilt top. Stitch one long edge of pieced strip around quilt top, mitering corners neatly. Press opposite edge ¼" to wrong side and turn to back of quilt. Slip-stitch folded edge of binding to quilt backing.

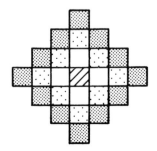

ASSEMBLY DIAGRAM FOR
TRIP AROUND
THE WORLD QUILT

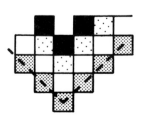

TRIMMING DIAGRAM

# Crocheted Pillowcase Edging

*Size:* 3¾" wide. Fits 40" case opening.

*Materials:* Size 30 crochet thread, 1 ball White. Steel crochet hook size 9.

*Gauge:* 11 mesh (dc, ch 2) = 2"; 6 rows = 1".

*Edging:* Ch 36. **Row 1:** Dc in 5th ch from hook, dc in next 6 ch, * ch 2, sk 2 ch, dc in 4 ch; rep from * across. Ch 3, turn. **Row 2:** Dc in next 3 dc – beg bl over bl made; * 2 dc in next ch sp, dc in next dc – bl over sp made; ch 2, sk 2 dc, dc in next dc – sp over bl made; rep from * 3 times, dc in last 3 dc – end bl over bl made. Ch 5, turn. **Row 3:** Dc in first 4 dc – ch lp and beg bl made; * bl over sp, sp over bl; rep from * 3 times, dc in next 2 dc, dc in top of turning ch 3 – end bl made. Ch 8, turn. **Row 4:** Dc in 4th ch from hook, dc in next 4 ch, dc in next dc – 2 beg bl inc made; sp over bl; ch 2, sk 2 ch, dc in next dc – sp over sp made; 7 sps, end bl. Ch 5, turn. Continue to follow Rows 5–19 of chart; then rep Rows 2–19 of chart 12 times more or desired length to fit case, end with a Row 18. Fasten off.

*Finishing:* Sew narrow ends of edging tog. Sew ch 5 lps of long edge to case edge.

## PILLOWCASE EDGING DIAGRAM

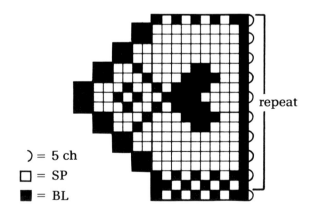

repeat

) = 5 ch
□ = SP
■ = BL

## Quilt Remnant Pillow

*Size:* 18″ square.

*Materials:* Cotton fabrics 44″–45″ wide: Tan print (T1), ⅝ yd.; a second tan print (T2), ¼ yd.; scraps of a third tan print (T3), a pink print (P), and a navy print (N); white sailcloth, 12″ square. Narrow cotton cording, 3⅜ yd. White sewing thread. 18″ square pillow form.

*Directions:* Read "General Directions for Quilting" on page 152. From first tan print (T1), cut two 19″ squares; set aside for pillow background and backing. From T2, cut 1½″ wide strips on the bias, enough to total 125″ in length; set aside for cording. Trace actual-size pattern for patch and make template. Use to cut 4 each from T1 and N, 8 each from T2, T3, and P. Also cut 2⅛″ squares: 4 from T1, 4 from N.

Stitch patches into large diamonds as follows, referring to assembly diagram: For Diamond I, first stitch an N to a T2 along seam a, forming a parallelogram. In same manner, stitch a T2 to a T3 (seam b). Stitch parallelograms together along long edges (seam c). Stitch 3 more Diamond I configurations. Next, create Diamond II, stitching a T1 to a P (seam d), a P to a T3 (seam e), and the two resulting parallelograms together along seam f. Make three more Diamond IIs in this manner. Stitch a Diamond I to each Diamond II along seam g. Place all 4 pieces together with g seams leading to center and diamonds creating the arms of an 8-pointed star. Taking care to match seams, stitch top two together, stitch bottom two together, then stitch top row to bottom row. Pin, centered, on white square. On all N and T1 squares, turn edges ¼″ to wrong side and press. Tuck squares between diamonds as shown on diagram. Slip-stitch all around 8-pointed star shape, and around each square patch.

*Assembly: Make cording:* stitch bias strips end to end. Place cotton cording on wrong side, lengthwise down center, and bring long edges of strips together to encase cording. Stitch, using zipper foot on sewing machine to get as close as possible to cotton cording.

Pin cording around patchwork square on right side, with cording seam touching tips of star points and raw edges facing outside. Stitch, again with zipper foot, close to cording. Where ends of cording meet, open out fabric around cording, cut cotton cord ends so they butt, overlap fabric edges neatly, and complete stitching cording in place. In same manner, stitch cording around background T1 square. Center white square on top, tucking seam allowances of white square and cording underneath. Slip-stitch in place along outside edge of cording.

Stitch background square and backing squares together along 3 sides. Clip corners, turn to right side, and insert pillow form. Slip-stitch fourth side closed.

ACTUAL-SIZE
PATTERN FOR PATCH

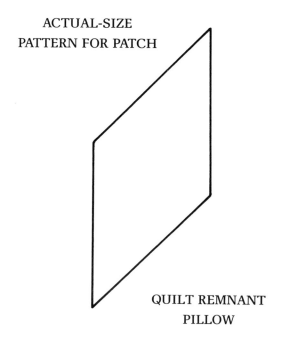

QUILT REMNANT
PILLOW

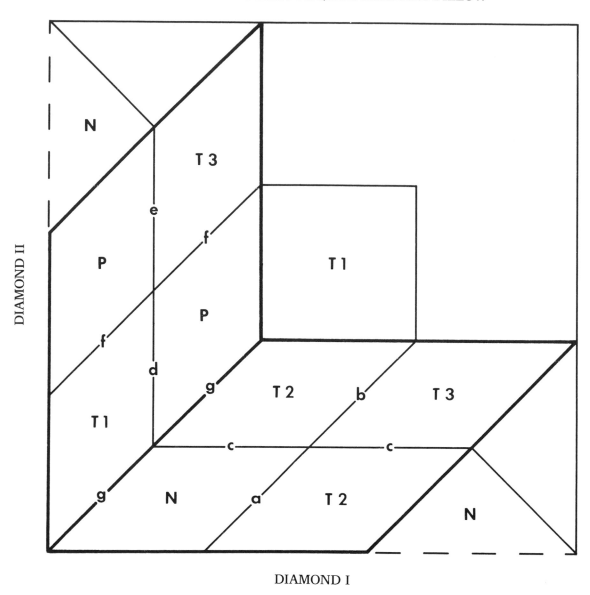

# Fraktur: Watercolor Certificate

**Size:** Design area, 13″ × 8⅜″.

**Materials:** Tracing paper. Graphite paper. White watercolor paper. Brown and black fine-tip permanent ink marking pens. Watercolor paints: rose (1), yellow ochre (2), blue (3), moss green. Fine-tip paintbrush.

**Directions:** Trace actual-size half pattern onto tracing paper. On watercolor paper, mark a 13″ × 8⅜″ rectangle for design; lightly pencil a vertical line down center of paper. Center pattern on left half of watercolor paper, with dash line on penciled center line. Use graphite paper and sharp pencil to transfer all design lines; do not transfer numbers and short lines leading to numbers. Lift pattern and replace on right half in order to continue bottom border's trellis design across to right side of design area. Turn tracing to wrong side and place on right half of watercolor paper; align dash lines at center. Transfer all but ¼″ of design to right of center and bottom border already marked. If desired, use eraser and pencil to change flowers on right half to correspond to actual piece; give flowers under heart serrated instead of scalloped petals; omit stamens on flowers above heart, and vary curlicues of tendrils, so design is somewhat less symmetrical.

To paint certificate, use just enough water to thin watercolors to a pale wash, but not so much that paints run or bleed. Shade leaves, flowers, and berries with strokes of stronger, less diluted hues of the same color. Paint all leaves, stems, and tendrils green, shading leaves with darker green. Paint flowers, berries, heart borders, and certificate borders, referring to numbers on pattern and materials list for colors. Paint border flowers rose. On right half of certificate, paint vertical oval rose, and serrated petaled flowers blue with yellow ochre accents.

Ink in all design lines using black fine-tip pen. Lightly pencil lettering onto certificate, then go over lines with brown fine-tip pen. Here are some suggestions for writing your cerificate: Inside hearts is a passage from Psalm 121 of the Bible; write a verse or song lyric of your own choosing. At top rectangle within yellow ochre stripes write your first and middle name, at bottom rectangle write last name. In spaces of interlocked ovals at center of certificate write names, events, and dates of importance to you.

Mat and frame certificate as desired.

**ACTUAL-SIZE PATTERN FOR FRAKTUR WATERCOLOR CERTIFICATE**

PATTERN FOR SONGBIRD HOOKED RUG   Each square = 1"

## Songbird Hooked Rug

**Size:** 30″ × 57″.

Read and refer to "General Directions for Hooked Rugs" on page 153. Enlarge pattern on paper ruled into 1″ squares. Work flowers with two shades of rose or blue in solids; more elaborate flowers include outlines of tweed in the same color family. Foliage combines sage green veins and olive leaves and stems. Each bird combines 2-3 muted tones of a different color: lavender, green, brown, and rose. If desired, place your initials in the vase. Separating grid and border is brown tweed. Background is a solid, even beige.

# Hovering Hawks Quilt

**Size:** 84½" × 95".

**Materials:** Cotton fabrics, 44" wide: various prints on white background, 4 yds. total; rose print (D), 2⅝ yds.; black print (A), 1 yd.; coral (B), ½ yd.; orange print (C), ⅜ yd.; small amounts of several other colors totaling 5½ yds.; fabric for backing, 5½ yds. White sewing and quilting thread. Quilt batting.

**Directions:** Read "General Directions for Quilting" on page 152. From rose print, cut strips: two 2¾" × 86½", two 2¾" × 93"; set aside for borders.

*Patches:* On graph paper, mark a 1¾" square. Divide in half diagonally, and make a template from resulting triangle. Use template to cut triangles as follows; refer to materials list for fabric type: 2392 from white print fabrics, 256 from A, 124 from B, 106 from C, 252 from D. Using remnants of these and any other fabrics on hand, cut out 1636 more triangles, all in groups of four from the same fabric.

*Quilt Top:* Quilt top is made up of 4784 triangular patches, sewn into squares which are then sewn together. A design results, first, from every square featuring a white print triangle in the upper right half, and secondly, from an inner area of concentric rectangles with specific color combinations, surrounded by an area of more random color placements.

To make squares, stitch a triangle with a white print to a colored triangle along their long edges. Assemble squares for inner area; refer to assembly diagram: For innermost rectangle, stitch 24 squares using A. For surrounding rectangle, use 24 B. For next rounds, use 32 A, then 40 C, then 48 A, then 56 D, then 64 A, then 152 rose, then 88 black, then 100 each coral and rose. Lay out as shown in assembly diagram; alternate or randomly space coral and rose patches in last round. Turn all squares so white print is at upper right. Assemble inner area: stitch squares into horizontal rows, then stitch rows together, taking care to match seams.

Assemble remaining triangles into 8-patch blocks: Stitch triangles in same white print to 4 triangles in same colored print. Lay out in 2 rows of 2, with white print triangles always at upper right. Stitch squares in each row together, then stitch row 1 to row 2. Stitch blocks together in four sections. Sections 1 and 4 feature 6 rows of 23 blocks. Sections 2 and 3 feature 14 rows of 5 blocks. Strive for a pleasing arrangement of colors. Stitch blocks in each row of section, then stitch rows together. Stitch completed Sections 2 and 3 to either side of inner area, then stitch Sections 1 and 4 to top and bottom.

*Assembly:* Stitch longer border strips to sides of quilt top, then stitch shorter strips to top and bottom. Piece backing, and layer with batting and quilt top, following General Directions.

*To Quilt:* Beginning at approximately the center of quilt, work a pattern of concentric diamonds, following diagram. Continue in pattern over borders.

*Bind Quilt:* Cut backing and batting even with quilt top. From remaining rose print, cut 1" strips on the bias totaling 10 yds. Stitch to edges of quilt top (borders), mitering corners. Turn opposite edge to backing, turn raw edge under ¼", and slip-stitch in place.

ASSEMBLY DIAGRAM FOR INNER AREA

□ = ◨

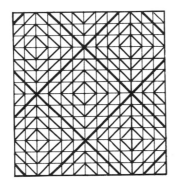

QUILTING DIAGRAM

# Painted Floorcloth

**Size:** 37" × 46".

**Materials:** Natural or white heavyweight cotton duck or pre-primed artist's canvas, 37" × 50". Craft glue. White flat latex paint. Acrylic paints in jars: yellow ochre, grass green, dark green, blue, pink, purple. Polyurethane varnish.

**Equipment:** Paint roller. Masking tape, ½" wide. Pencil. Yardstick. Tracing paper. Graphite paper. Dry ball-point pen. Paintbrushes: Round tapered and fine liner. Iron. Spray starch.

**Directions:** *Prepare surface:* To smooth away wrinkles from canvas, iron with spray starch. Turn short edges 2" to wrong side and hem by gluing down. Spread newspaper under floorcloth and apply 2 or 3 coats of white paint with a roller, running over the edges to seal all threads. Let each coat dry completely before applying next coat. Reserve some paint for touch-ups. Lightly pencil lines lengthwise and widthwise along center of cloth, dividing it into 4 quadrants. For border stripes, place masking tape along short ends, 2½" and again 3⅝" from edge. Dilute yellow ochre with water and paint a light wash of color between strips of tape. Let dry, then remove tape.

*Prepare and Transfer Patterns:* Enlarge patterns on large sheets of tracing paper ruled into 1" squares. Center motif is a quarter pattern, side border is a half pattern, as indicated by long dash lines. Transfer patterns to cloth as follows: Hold cloth with short edges at sides, long edges at top and bottom. Place center motif in upper right quad-

QUARTER PATTERN FOR CENTER MOTIF    Each square = 1″

rant of cloth, lining up corner of dash lines with center and dash lines along pencil lines. Tape to secure, insert graphite paper, and go over all design lines with dry ball-point pen, to transfer pattern. Turn tracing to wrong side and transfer pattern in reverse to upper left quadrant. Turn cloth around and repeat. Turn cloth so short edges are at top and bottom. Tape border motif to bottom edge, so lowest open circle is ¾″ from yellow stripe and dash line is on penciled lengthwise center line. Transfer, then turn pattern to wrong side and transfer left half in reverse, for mirror image. Turn cloth around and transfer border to other short side in same manner. Also transfer corner motif as shown in bracketed area to either side of crosswise center, placing pattern with stamens touching penciled line and 3¼″ from edge of cloth, and reversing pattern for mirror image. Extend vines from border motifs in a graceful curve along sides of cloth; refer to photo on page 100.

*To Paint Design:* Read painting directions for "Folk Art Oil Paintings" on page 130. Practice teardrop stroke and outlining. Use these techniques to paint design in colors as follows: Paint stamens, open circles, and bird beaks yellow. Add two yellow teardrop curves above each side motif. Paint birds blue. Paint flowers shown shaded on pattern at center of border pink, paint all other shaded flowers purple, mixing a bit of blue on brush for borders. Paint vines with grass green, thinned with a little water; paint leaves with varying tones of dark green, taking a bit of yellow on brush for some of the leaves.

*Finishing:* Vacuum cloth and dust with a clean tack cloth. Apply 3 coats of varnish, letting each coat dry and dusting with a tack cloth before applying the next coat.

PATTERN FOR PAINTED FLOORCLOTH

CORNER MOTIF

HALF PATTERN FOR BORDER MOTIF  Each square = 1"

# Band Box

*Size:* 6″ in diameter; 2½″ high.

*Materials:* Oaktag, 12″ × 20″ rectangle. Medium to heavy-weight wrapping paper, or wallpaper (not vinyl). Newspaper. Masking tape. Spray adhesive. Clear acrylic sealer.

*Equipment:* Pencil. Tracing paper. Graphite paper. Scissors. Xacto knife or mat knife. Ruler.

*Directions:* On tracing paper, trace actual-size pattern for box (solid lines) and, on a separate piece of paper, lid (short dash lines). Complete quarter pattern, as indicated by long dash lines. Tape patterns to oaktag, and using graphite (or carbon) paper, transfer all lines. Cut out oaktag box and lid along outlines. Using a ruler and an Xacto knife, score lines of octagons— for bottom of box, top of lid. To score, draw knife along lines but do not cut all the way through oaktag. Turn oaktag over and fold sides of box and lid up

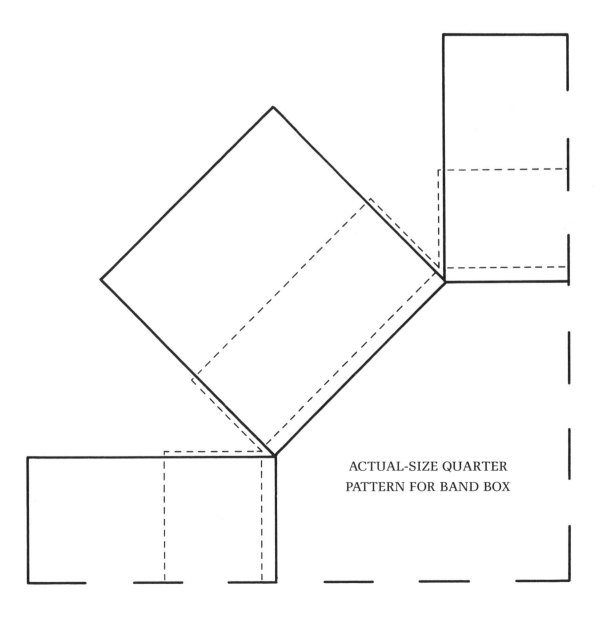

ACTUAL-SIZE QUARTER
PATTERN FOR BAND BOX

103

along scored lines. Tape sides together along edges.

Transfer octagonal shapes for box bottom and lid top to one sheet each decorative paper and newspaper; cut out. Also mark and cut rectangular strips: $3\frac{1}{4}'' \times 20\frac{1}{2}''$ and $1\frac{1}{2}'' \times 21''$ from decorative paper, $1\frac{3}{8}'' \times 20\frac{1}{2}''$ and $\frac{7}{8}'' \times 21''$ from newspaper. Spray wrong side of larger strip with adhesive, following manufacturer's instructions on can. Wrap strip around box, centering so $\frac{3}{8}''$ of paper extends beyond rim and bottom of box. Press paper smooth and flat as you go to avoid air bubbles. Overlap short edges. Clip into $\frac{3}{8}''$ extensions at each corner, then fold paper over rim to inside of box and to bottom of box. Spray larger newspaper strip and wrap around inside of box. Spray smaller newspaper octagon and apply to inside bottom of box; glue smaller octagon of decorative paper to outside bottom of box. In same manner, cover lid. Spray box and lid with 2 coats of clear acrylic sealer.

## Tea Cloth with Crocheted Edging

*Size:* 3½" wide. Fits a 26" square or a 26" × 34" cloth.

*Materials:* Size 30 crochet thread, 2 balls White. Steel crochet hook size 10. Cloth finished to 26" × 34" or a 26" square.

*Gauge:* 8 mesh (dc, ch 2) = 1"; 9 rows = 1".

*Edging:* Ch 67. **Row 1** (wrong side): Dc in 4 th ch from hook, dc in next 6 ch, ch 2, sk 2 ch, dc in next ch, ch 2, sk 2 ch, dc in next 7 ch, ch 2, sk 2 ch, sc in next ch, ch 2, sk 2 ch, dc in next 30 ch, ch 2, sk 2 ch, sc in next ch, ch 2, sk 2 ch, dc in next ch, ch 2, sk 2 ch, sc in next ch, ch 2, sk 2 ch, dc in last ch. Ch 8, turn. **Row 2:** Dc in next dc – beg long sp over V-Bl made; ch 5, sk next ch 2 and sc and ch 2, dc in next dc – long sp over V-Bl made; dc in next 30 dc – 10 bls over 10 bls made; long sp, dc in next 6 dc – 2 bls over 2 bls made; ch 2, sk 2 ch, dc in next dc, ch 2, sk 2 ch, dc in next dc – 2 sps over 2 sps made; dc in next 5 dc, dc in top of turning ch – 2 end bls over 2 end bls made. Ch 8, turn. **Row 3:** Dc in 4th ch from hook and in next 4 ch, dc in next dc – 2 bls inc made; ch 2, sk 2 dc, dc in next dc, ch 2, sk 2 dc, dc in next dc – 2 sps over 2 bls made; 2 dc in next sp, dc in dc, 2 dc in next sp, dc in dc – 2 bls over 2 sps made; ch 2, sk 2 dc, sc in next dc, ch 2, sk 2 dc, dc in next dc – V-Bl over 2 bls made; 5 dc in long sp, dc in next dc – 2 bls over long sp made; 5 V-Bl, 2 bls over long sp, ch 2, sc in center of long sp, ch 2, dc in 3rd ch of

long sp – V-Bl over end long sp made. Ch 8, turn. **Row 4:** Beg long sp over V-Bl, 2 bls over 2 bls, ch 5, dc in next dc – long sp over V-Bl made; 4 long sps, 2 bls, 1 long sp, 2 bls, 2 sps, 2 bls. Ch 8, turn. **Rows 5–8:** Follow chart. At end of last row ch 1, turn. **Row 9:** Sl st in 7 dc of beg 2 bls, ch 3, 2 dc in next sp, dc in next dc, 2 dc in next sp, dc in dc – dec over beg 2 bls and 2 bls over 2 sps made; 2 sps, 2 bls, (2 V-Bls, 2 bls) 3 times, end V-Bl. **Rows 10–24:** Follow chart. At end of last row ch 1, turn.

*Shape Corner: First Half:* **Row 1:** Dec over 2 bls, 2 bls, 2 sps, 2 bls, V-Bl, 10 sps, V-Bl; leave end long sp unworked – dec over end long sp made. Ch 8, turn. Follow chart for first half of corner through Row 24. Ch 8, turn to work along decs on edge of these 24 rows (mitre edge).
*Second Half:* **Row 25:** Dc in 4th ch from hook and in next 4 ch, dc in top of end dc of Row 24, ch 2, dc in top of end dc of Row 23, ch 2, dc in base of same dc of Row 23 – 2 sps made across ends of rows, 2 dc in each sp at ends of next 2 rows, dc in top of end dc of next row, join with sl st in center of long sp at end of next row, sl st to corner of same long sp, turn. Row 26: Work 2 bls over 2 bls of Row 25, 2 sps over 2 sps, 2 bls over 2 bls. Ch 1, turn. Follow chart for second half of corner through Row 47, joining ends of rows at mitre edge with sl st in long sps as before. **Rows 48–54:** Follow chart. Then rep Rows 1–12 of chart 19 times, end with Row 12. Work the 47 rows for another corner. Continue in this way for 4 corners and sides, end with Row 12 of chart. Fasten off.
*Finishing:* Sew ends tog. Sew edging to finished edges of fabric.

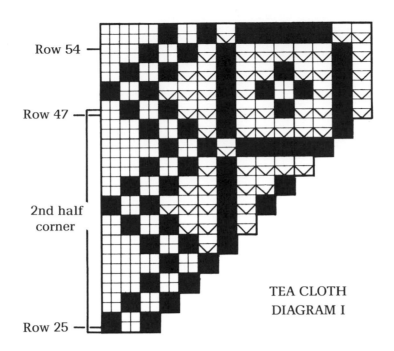

Row 54 —

Row 47 —

2nd half
corner

Row 25 —

TEA CLOTH
CROCHETED EDGING

TEA CLOTH
DIAGRAM I

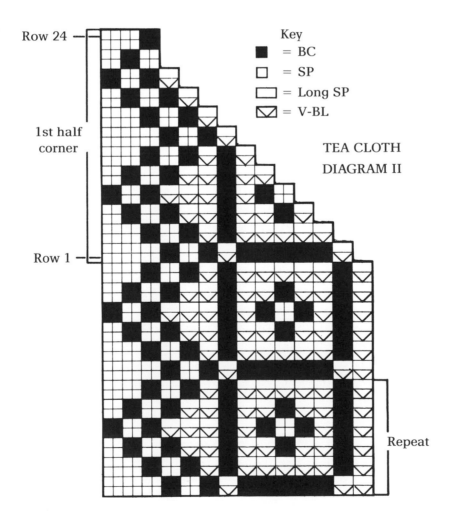

Row 24 —

1st half
corner

Row 1 —

Key
■ = BC
□ = SP
▭ = Long SP
◩ = V-BL

TEA CLOTH
DIAGRAM II

Repeat

107

# A Child's Room

**DOUBLE IRISH CHAIN QUILT**
**STUFFED ANIMALS**
**FOLK ART OIL PAINTINGS**
**PULL-TOY LAMB**
**TEA PARTY DOLL FURNITURE**
**VINE WREATH WITH HEARTS**
**GRETCHEN HOOKED RUG**

The children who lived on farms in early America did not have their own beds, much less their own bedrooms. Frequently they shared a room with brothers and sisters, and it was not uncommon for a number of siblings to sleep in one double bed. In the converted attic of this restored 18th-century house, a charming young person's room has all the trappings of an old-fashioned country bedroom—to be enjoyed in modern times.

The cornflower-blue-and-white antique quilt is the Double Irish Chain pattern. It has the disciplined harmony that most geometrics exude, and I am quite partial to them. Huddled together on the bed pillow is a collection of well-loved stuffed animals—a floppy-eared mother rabbit with baby, which was designed by Heidi Steiner of Wisconsin; my fleecy lamb in a party dress; and my miniature bunny family in their Sunday best. Looking on from a colorful ladderback chair is my hound dog in a smoking jacket, reading the newspaper. What I find so enchanting about this group of stuffed animals is their understated humor.

Working in the style of early limners, a contemporary folk artist, The Jersey Limner, has painted a portrait of a gentle lamb entitled *Sheep Farm*. The landscape appears distorted in shape and perspective, and a modern house seems oddly out of place. However, we know that these characteristics are typical of early work and that the limners of the past juxtaposed non-related objects for the sake of composition; they were noted for adding bowls of succulent strawberries if they wanted a splash of vibrant color. Contemporary limners, such as The Jersey Limner, have developed personal folk painting styles but have stayed close to the folk art painting tradition. Thus, their pictures are reminiscent of the flat, distorted, and often witty work of earlier artists. *Goose Farm* depicts two large, misshapen geese paused, it seems, to take an appraising look at the curious limner (page 133). Elongated trees and ominous shadows create a surreal atmosphere, while the naiveté and inherent humor of this painting draw us back to old traditions.

On the windowsill sit Bo Peep Bear with her lamb and Dassey Bear with quilt; both were designed by Tammie Lawrence of Wisconsin. The brightly painted figure of a man was constructed from wood scraps by my daughter Gabrielle when she was five years old, and the architectural model of a house was made by my daughter Genevieve (page 126).

Folk artists create from a personal point of view and in terms of what has meaning for them. The animals and dolls in this collection express the sentiments of their creators. Mothers throughout the ages have cut and stitched toys for their children; they have replaced threadbare countenances with new ones. They have saved toys as they would their favorite china.

Mothers were not the only ones, however, who were involved in creating magical playthings from scrap. Unidentified carpenters and other craftsmen have over the years left countless whirligigs, checkerboards, rocking horses, and pull toys for children. In the spirit of the wooden version of the pull-toy lamb, soft sculpture folk designer Beverly Karcher, from New Jersey, combined the soft lamb toy with commercially produced wheels to create this pull-toy lamb (page 136). Though the original religious significance of the "Lamb of God" may have been forgotten, many folk artists continue to feature this animal in their work.

Arranged for a delightful tea party, these stuffed animals are sturdy toys for children. Seated around a miniature set of doll furniture made by LeRoy Zeigler, a menagerie of eccentric guests enjoy watermelon and tea (page 6). One can just imagine the conversation! Karen Meer of Wisconsin designed the folk horse dolls, and Heidi Steiner created and stitched the black cat in party dress and apron. An antique doll's apron is framed and hung on the wall, as is a miniature sampler.

Here again is the favorite motif of folk artists—the heart. Scattered around this simple vine wreath, the bright-red hearts amongst a few dried flowers add a loving touch to the room (page 146).

A charming example of the simple floral patterns of early 19th-century hooked rugs is Marion N. Ham's creation, called Gretchen (page 147). Six blocks contain sweet bouquets of pastel blue and pink flowers; a thick chain border encloses the blocks, giving the overall impression of a bed quilt.

## Double Irish Chain Quilt

*Size:* Approximately 69" × 85".

*Materials:* Cotton fabrics, 44" wide: white, 9 yds.; blue, 3 yds. White sewing and quilting thread. Quilt batting. White quilt binding, 8½ yds.

*Directions:* Read "General Directions for Quilting" on page 152. From white fabric, cut two 88" lengths across full width of fabric; set aside for backing and outer borders. From blue fabric, cut 2 strips 1⅞" × 82", two 1⅞" × 71"; set aside for inner borders.

*Patches:* Using graph paper, make templates for a 3" square and a 1" square. Use templates to cut the following: from white fabric, 166 large squares, 1477 small squares; from blue fabric, 1610 small squares.

*Quilt Blocks:* Large white squares form an entire quilt block, to be referred to as Block A. Piece small squares into 9-patch blocks, consisting of 3 rows of 3. For Block B, place blue squares at corners and center, white at center of each side; see key. Block C is the reverse of Block B: place a white square at corners and center, a blue square at the center of each side. Stitch squares into rows, then stitch rows together, taking care to match seams, for each complete B and C block.

*Quilt Top:* Turn assembly diagram so upper left corner is at top. Referring to key, lay out quilt blocks A, B, and C as shown, from Row 1 to Row 16. Note that rows progressively increase by one block on each side until Row 16, which increases on the left, but decreases on the right. Stitch blocks together in each row, then stitch rows together, taking care to match seams. Turn assembly

diagram around so lower right corner is at top. In same manner as before, assemble Rows 16–32. Pin Row 32 to Row 16 as shown; stitch together, taking care to match seams.

*Borders:* Cut one large piece of white fabric reserved for backing lengthwise in half. Cut a 2" × 71" and a 2" × 82" strip along selvage of each half, for outer borders.

Pin a long blue border strip to either long edge (side) of quilt top. Stitch diagonally through outside quilt blocks, as indicated by dash line on assembly diagram. Stitch a white 80" strip to either side of blue strip. Trim ends of these strips even with pointed edge along top and bottom of quilt top. Pin remaining blue strips to top and bottom of quilt, and stitch along dash lines as before. Add remaining white outer border strips to top and bottom of quilt. Trim ends of top and bottom border strips even with long edges of side borders.

*Assembly:* Piece backing by stitching remaining halves of white fabric to either side of largest white piece. Layer batting on wrong side of backing, and center quilt top, right side up on top.

*Quilting:* Use quilting thread, and start from the center and work outwards. Quilt each Quilt Block A as follows: stitch ¼" within seams all around. Holding block with upper left edge at the top, quilt vertically into thirds, or at 1" intervals. Extend these stitches across into side borders, and quilt top and bottom borders vertically at the same intervals, to correspond. Next, quilt diagonally through centers of all small squares, so stitching goes horizontally across quilt.

*Binding:* Bind quilt with white quilt binding, following manufacturer's instructions.

## ASSEMBLY DIAGRAM FOR DOUBLE IRISH CHAIN QUILT

☐ = Quilt Block A (large white square)

▧ = Quilt Block B

◼ = Quilt Block C

## Mother Rabbit with Baby

*Size:* 14½″ tall, with ears flopped down.

*Materials:* Cotton fabrics 44″–45″ wide: Muslin, ⅜ yd.; blue plaid cotton print, ¼ yd. Matching thread. Lace trim ¾″ wide, ⅜ yd. Small amount of white pearl cotton. Cotton twill tape ¾″ wide, ¾ yd. Polyester fiberfill.

*Directions: Rabbit:* Read and refer to "General Directions for Stuffed Animals and Dolls" on page 154. Use patterns to cut 2 head/bodies, 4 ears, 4 arms, 4 legs from muslin. Stitch ears, arms, and legs together in matching pairs, leaving short straight edges unstitched. Turn pieces to right sides. Press ears, and baste a pleat at center of short edge, narrowing edge to ⅝″. Pin ears to top of one head piece, ½″ apart. Stitch head/bodies together, taking care to catch ends but not sides of ears in stitching, and leaving areas unstitched between dots and along straight bottom edge. Turn to right side. Stuff arms and legs to within 1″ of openings. Turn body edges between dots ¼″ to inside, and insert arms, with thumb seams at center front; stitch. Stuff head/body to within ½″ of opening, and turn raw edges ¼″ to inside. Insert legs with seams at center front and back, toes facing forward (same as thumbs). Stitch across bottom of body.

*Dress:* From blue plaid fabric, cut one bodice/sleeves piece, using pattern, plus a 7½″ × 21¾″ rectangle, for skirt. Make dress same as for Black Cat, page 142.

*Bloomers:* Make same as for Black Cat, with the following exceptions: clean-finish waist and leg edges, instead of making casings. Trim leg edges with lace, and make running stitches with pearl cotton across waist and legs; pull to gather.

*Apron:* Cut a 6¼″ × 8″ rectangle from muslin. Press short sides ¼″ to wrong side. Hem one long (bottom) edge; gather opposite (top) edge to 3¾″. Stitch center of twill tape across top edge.

*Baby:* From muslin, cut 2 baby bodies, 4 baby ears, using patterns, plus a 3″ × 7″ rectangle, for a swaddling blanket. Stitch ears together in pairs, leaving open along straight edges. Turn, press, and baste side by side to narrow (head) end of one baby body. Stitch bodies together, taking care not to catch sides of ears in stitching, and leaving straight edge unstitched. Turn, stuff, and slip-stitch opening closed. Turn one long edge of blanket ⅝″ to right side, and short edges 1″ to wrong side; press. Place baby on wrong side of blanket at center, with head end extending ¾″ beyond long folded edge. Turn opposite long edge over front of baby, then fold sides to front, turning top corners down for ½″. Tack to secure. Tack baby in swaddling blanket to Mother Rabbit's apron waistband.

*Finishing:* "Antique" and mottle all pieces, following "General Directions for Stuffed Animals and Dolls."

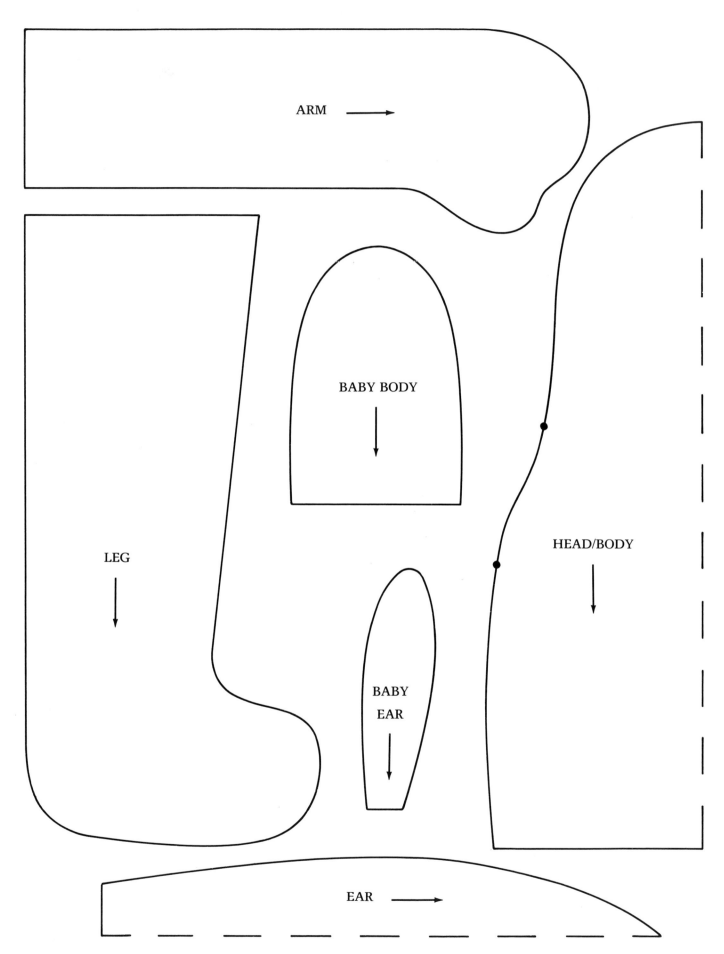

ARM

BABY BODY

LEG

HEAD/BODY

BABY
EAR

EAR

ACTUAL-SIZE PATTERNS FOR MOTHER RABBIT AND BABY

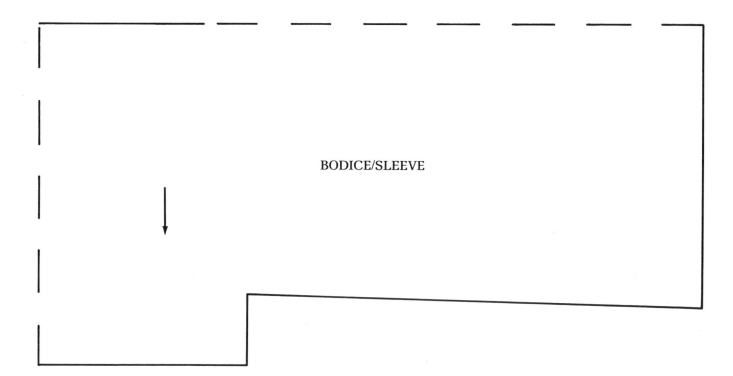

BODICE/SLEEVE

115

ACTUAL-SIZE DIAGRAM FOR HOUND DOG'S SPECTACLES

## *Hound Dog and Party Lamb*

**Sizes:** Dog, 17¼" tall; Lamb, 15".

**Materials:** Scraps of muslin fabric. Black acrylic paint. Sewing thread to match fabrics. Polyester fiberfill.
*For Dog:* Tan wool fabric 36" wide, ⅜ yd. Striped velveteen 36" wide, ⅜ yd. Scrap of red polyester satin fabric. Copper wire. Newspaper.
*For Lamb:* Pink fleece fabric 36" wide, ⅜ yd, or two 12" × 18" rectangles. Floral cotton fabric 44" wide, ⅜ yd. Floral print handkerchief, approximately 11" square.

**Directions:** Read and refer to "General Directions for Stuffed Animals and Dolls" on page 154. Using patterns, and tan wool for dog or pink fleece for lamb, cut 2 body pieces, 2 arms, 2 legs, 2 ears. Also for dog, cut a 1⅜" × 7" rectangle, for tail. Use appropriate ear pattern and muslin fabric to cut 2 inner ears for either animal.
*For Dog Tail:* Turn long edges ¼" to wrong side, then fold lengthwise in half, encasing a 7" length of wire; whip-stitch edges together.

For either animal, stitch matching body pieces together along all but straight bottom edge; insert Dog's tail at bottom of center back seam. Pinch muzzle ⅝" from top curve and tack to form nose. Turn to right side; stuff. For Lamb, clip fleece within dotted line on pattern to define area of muzzle. For either animal, paint eyes. For Dog, tack a stitch at one eye, pull through head to other eye, and repeat, pulling thread taut each time to sink eyes into face. Stitch an outer ear to an inner ear along all but the narrowest (top) end. Turn to right side, turn open end ¼" to inside and tack to head: For Dog, use fine curved line for ear placement; for Lamb, pinch ends of ears to curl, use dot-dash line on pattern to guide placement, and stitch ears facing front.

Fold each arm and leg lengthwise in half along long dash line; stitch along all but short straight (top) edge. Turn and stuff. With seams in front, attach arms to sides of body, legs to bottom of body ⅜" from sides and ⅞" apart.
*Dog's Smoking Jacket and Finishing Details:* Use patterns and velveteen fabric to cut 1 jacket, 1 facing, 2 sleeves; also cut one 2" × 18" rectangle for belt. For each sleeve, stitch long edges together; clean-finish short straight edges. Slit armholes in jacket where indicated. Pin sleeves to armholes with highest curve of sleeve (cap) at top and seam at back; slit armhole a little further if necessary. Stitch. Pin shawl collar facing to curved top edge of jacket;

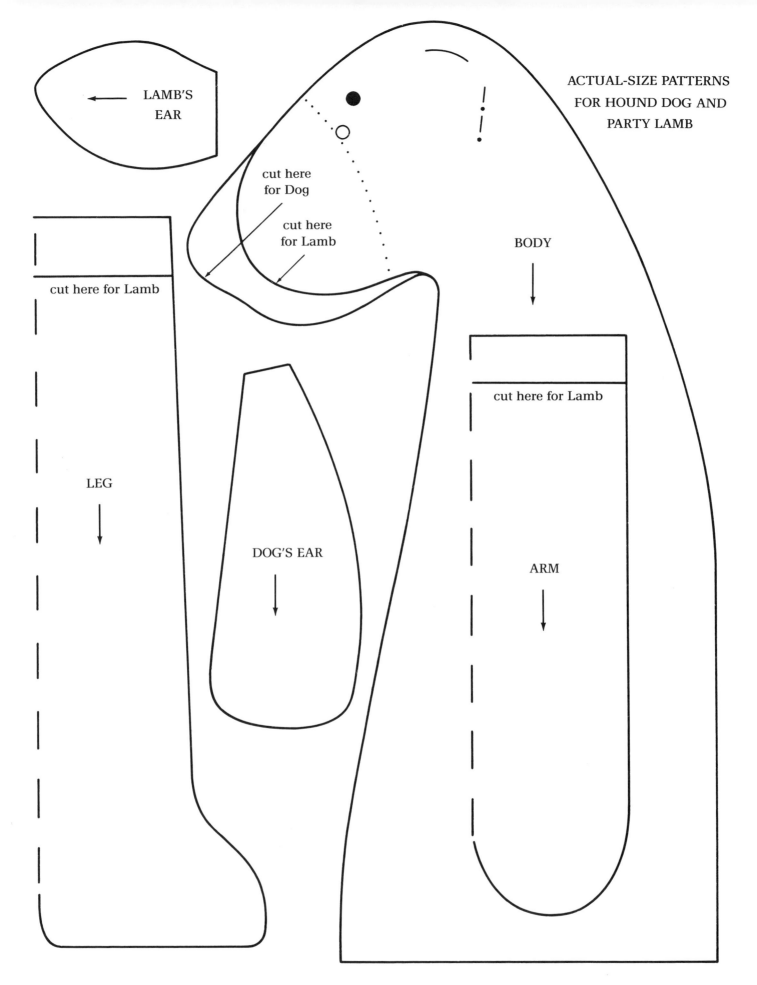

LAMB'S
EAR

ACTUAL-SIZE PATTERNS
FOR HOUND DOG AND
PARTY LAMB

cut here
for Dog

cut here
for Lamb

cut here for Lamb

BODY

cut here for Lamb

LEG

DOG'S EAR

ARM

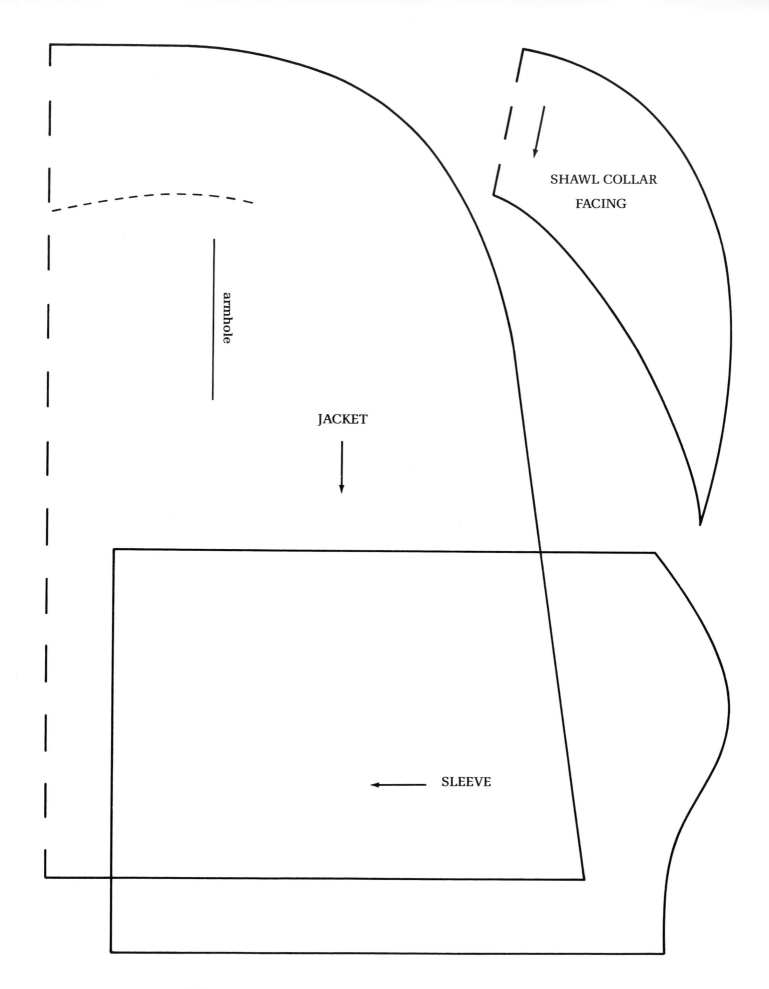

armhole

JACKET

SHAWL COLLAR
FACING

SLEEVE

118

stitch and turn facing to inside. Gather jacket along short dash lines. Turn inside edge of facing to inside and slipstitch to jacket. Turn front edges of jacket ⅜″ to inside. Hem bottom edge. For belt, turn edges ¼″ to wrong side, fold lengthwise in half and topstitch all around. Slip jacket on dog, overlap front edges, and belt to secure.

*Ascot:* From paper, cut a 9½″ square and cut diagonally in half. Use one of the resulting triangles as a pattern to cut ascot from satin polyester fabric. Narrowly hem edges. Tie around Dog's neck.

*Spectacles:* Cut a 9¼″ length of copper wire. Following actual-size diagram, bend into shape. Perch on muzzle, fold stems straight back, and insert through weave of fabric into head, under ears.

*Newspaper:* Cut 15 5¼″ × 8″ rectangles from newspaper. Fold crosswise in half. Tack center of short edges through all layers to paws.

*Lamb's Dress:* From floral fabric, cut rectangles: 14″ × 9½″, for bodice, 5¼″ × 21½″, for flounce, 1½″ × 33″, for ruffle, and two 4¾″ × 5¼″, for sleeves. Fold bodice crosswise in half; seam, forming a tube. Clean-finish one (top) edge. Hem one long edge of both flounce and ruffle. Gather other long edge of ruffle. Pin wrong side of ruffle to right side of flounce and distribute gathers evenly; stitch to secure. Bring short edges of ruffle/flounce together and stitch. Gather ruffled edge of flounce to fit bottom edge of bodice; pin, matching seams, and stitch. Fold each sleeve crosswise in half; seam. Clean-finish and gather one end, then turn other end under ¼″ and press. Place dress on Lamb with bodice seam at center back. Tack top edges together close to neck, and pull arms through remaining openings at sides. Slide on sleeves, and tack pressed-under edges to bodice. Fold handkerchief diagonally in half and tie about Lamb's neck.

# Miniature Bunny Family

**Size:** Mama, Papa, 6½″, Baby, 2½″.

**Materials:** Unbleached muslin 36″ wide, ¼ yd. Small amounts of fabrics: white, blue, blue calico, pink print. Scrap of white felt. Thread to match fabrics. Polyester fiberfill. Red acrylic paint. Pink crayon. Scrap of ¾″-wide white eyelet. Tiny silk flower. Seed beads: 6 black, 3 white, 4 blue, 9 turquoise. Black felt-tip pen.

**Directions:** Read and refer to "General Directions for Stuffed Animals and Dolls" on page 154. From muslin, use patterns to cut 2 large bodies and 4 ears for each adult bunny; cut 2 small bodies for baby. To assemble each bunny, stitch bodies together around sides and top, leaving bottom open. Turn to right side. With body flattened in profile, transfer eye and mouth markings to each half of bunny. Baste around body opening, ¼″ from bottom. Stuff bunny with fiberfill; pull gathering threads to close opening and stitch across bottom to secure. Sew black seed beads over eyes of adults, passing thread back and forth through head and tugging to sink eye areas; for baby, draw "dot" eyes with black felt-tipped pen. Backstitch on nose and mouth lines through stuffing, pinching in fabric and pulling thread to shape face. "Rouge" muzzle with crayon. For whiskers on adults, pass doubled thread back and forth through muzzle area, leaving loops on either side; cut loops. Stitch adult ears together in pairs around curved edges, leaving bottom open. Clip curves, turn and flatten each ear; color inside of ear with crayon as shown. For baby, cut 2 ears from felt, using pattern. Slip-stitch ears to crown of head; pleat bottoms of adult ears in center as shown, before stitching. Paint "dot" mouth on each, using tiny paintbrush and red acrylic paint. For Mama's arms and Papa's hands, cut 4 from muslin, using pattern. Pair pieces and stitch around, leaving flat end (top) open. Turn, stuff, and slip-stitch opening closed. Insert into sleeves as directed below and stitch in place.

*Papa Bunny:* Using pattern, cut 4 feet from muslin. Stitch together in pairs, leaving top open; turn and stuff. Slip-stitch opening closed; with toes forward, tack tops to sides of body. *Shirt:* From white fabric, cut 4 collars and 2½″ × 5″ rectangle; clean-finish edges. With long edges at top and bottom, and top edge even with Papa's "neck," wrap piece around torso, overlapping ends at center back; slip-stitch ends in place; sew 3 white seed bead "buttons" down back. Pair collars and stitch around outside (curved) edge; clip curves and turn; press under inside edge ¼″ to make tab. Position collar pieces on each side of shirt's center front, pushing tabs under neck edge; pin; slip-stitch all around, catching in tabs. From white fabric, cut two 2½″ × 4½″ rectangles for sleeves; press long edges ¼″ to wrong side. Fold each in half widthwise and stitch short edges together to make tube; turn; baste ⅛″ in from each end of tube. Gather one end closed, making top of sleeve; slip-stitch to shirt at "shoulders"; lightly stuff sleeve with fiberfill. Make hands; insert ¼″ of hand inside cuff; pull basting thread and gather cuff to fit wrist; slip-stitch all around.

*Trousers and Suspenders:* Using pattern, cut 2 trousers from blue fabric; also cut two 1″ × 4″ rectangles, for suspender straps. Stitch trouser pieces together along front and back seams (curved edges). Press waist (A) and cuffs (B) ¼″ to wrong side; stitch waist

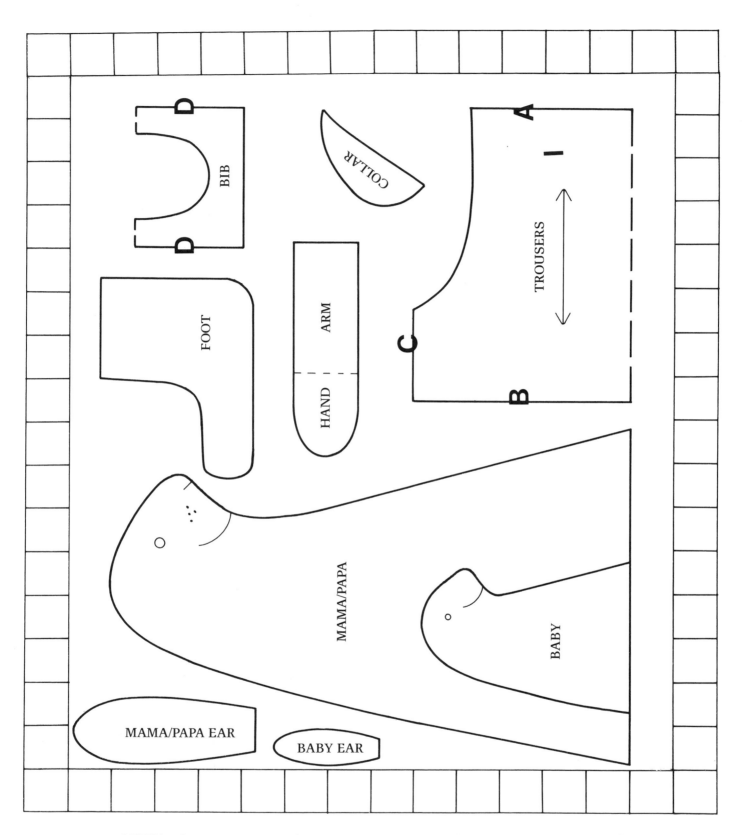

ACTUAL-SIZE PATTERNS FOR MINIATURE BUNNY FAMILY    Each square = 1″

⅛" in from crease all around, then baste cuffs ⅛" in from crease. Align front and back seams and stitch across inseam (C). Turn trousers to right side and place on Papa. Gather cuffs to fit legs. Double-fold straps lengthwise and top-stitch close to creases. Place trousers on Papa and tack ends of straps inside waist, drawing straps over shoulders and crossing them in back. Stitch 2 black seed bead "buttons" to trousers just below front suspenders.

*Mama Bunny: Dress:* Cut a 4½" × 18" rectangle of blue calico; hem long sides; press. Fold piece in half crosswise, right side in, and stitch short sides together to make tube; press seam open; turn. Baste ⅛" and ¾" in from one (top) edge all around; place Mama in tube and pull basting threads, gathering top to fit "neck" and bottom thread to fit "waist." For sleeves, cut two 1" × 2½" pieces of blue calico; clean-finish edges of short sides. Fold each piece in half lengthwise and stitch long edges together to make tube; turn and stuff. Make hands. Place wrists inside sleeves; slip-stitch. Stitch sleeves to dress at "shoulders."

*Pinafore:* Cut 2 bibs and 4¾" × 14" rectangle for skirt from white fabric. Place bibs together and stitch around neck edge. Slit bib open from one short end (bottom of back) to neckline; turn. Turn side edges (D) and slit back edges of both bib pieces ¼" to inside and top-stitch. Hem short edges and one long edge (bottom). If desired, change sewing machine setting to decorative stitch and topstitch bottom hem, using blue thread. Press top edge of skirt ¼" to wrong side and gather to an 8" width; stitch along basting. Pin bottom of bib front to skirt, matching centers; stitch along bottom of bib. Pin top corners of skirt to bib back; stitch along bottom of bib. Stitch 4 blue seed bead "buttons" along back bib. Place pinafore on bunny.

*Finishing Details:* Cut 4" piece of ¾" wide eyelet for cap; gather bound or raw edge to fit around head just under ears; slip-stitch in place. Tack small silk flower between ears. String 9 turquoise beads and stitch in circle at neckline center, for brooch.

*For Baby Bunny:* Cut a 5" square of pink calico and wrap baby as shown. Place baby in Mama's arms and tack hands to blanket.

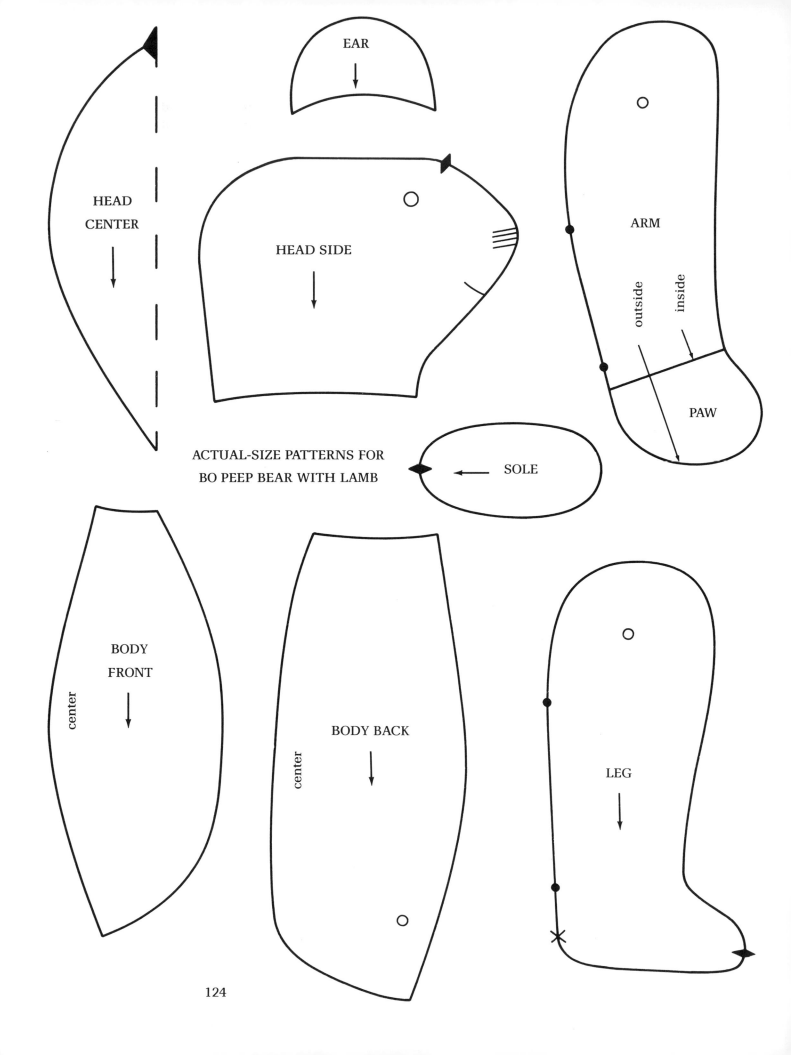

EAR

HEAD
CENTER

HEAD SIDE

ARM

outside

inside

PAW

ACTUAL-SIZE PATTERNS FOR
BO PEEP BEAR WITH LAMB

SOLE

BODY
FRONT

center

BODY BACK

center

LEG

124

## Bo Peep Bear with Lamb

*Size:* 9¾″ tall.

*Materials:* Fabrics: medium-weight tan wool melton or brushed wool 36″ wide, ¼ yd.; scraps of ecru; striped toweling fabric 18″ wide, ¼ yd.; 9″ × 12″ rectangle blue baby gingham; scraps of black lightweight wool, off-white sherpa fleece. Thread to match fabrics. 2 sets of small doll joints. 2 black ¼″ beads. Black pearl cotton. Polyester fiberfill. Craft glue. Twig.

*Directions:* *Bear:* Read "General Directions for Stuffed Animals and Dolls" on page 154. Use patterns to cut the following pieces: from tan wool, 2 head sides, 1 head center, 4 ears, 2 body fronts, 2 body backs, 2 inside arms, 2 outside arms, 4 legs. From ecru wool, cut 2 paws, 2 soles.

Stitch head center to each head side, matching notches and stitching toward back of head. Stitch head sides together from notch to bottom of chin; leave head open along bottom edge. Stitch ears together in pairs, leaving bottom edges open. Stitch body fronts and backs together in pairs along their center edges. Stitch joined fronts to joined backs, leaving straight (top) edges unstitched. Stitch paws to inside arms, then stitch an inner arm to each outer arm, leaving open between dots. Stitch legs together in pairs, leaving open between dots, and between X mark and notch. Stitch a sole to bottom of each leg, matching notches.

Poke a small hole at each open circle. Turn head, ears, body, arms, and legs to right side; stuff head firmly, other pieces plumply. Insert male part of doll joints through holes in arms and legs from wrong sides; add stuffing to firm limbs and secure joints. Slip-stitch openings closed. Slide female part of doll joints between fiberfill and fabric and line up with holes in body. Clamp arms and legs to body, then add fiberfill to stuff body firmly. Turn neck edges of head and body to inside and slip-stitch together. Turn raw edges of each ear to inside. Pinch a pleat in center of each and stitch to top of head, centered over seam between head side and head center. Stitch a bead to one head side at eye placement indicated by large open circle; insert needle through head to other eye marking. Pull thread taut to sink eye into head. Repeat for second eye. Using pearl cotton, straight-stitch nose, mouth, and along seam in between.

*Clothing: Robe:* Use pattern to cut 2 from tea toweling, with stripes going vertically down robe. Stitch together along top and bottom edges of sleeves and sides of robe. Clean-finish neck edge and sleeve ends, then gather sleeve ends. Hem bottom edge.

*Bonnet:* Use patterns to cut 2 brims, one crown/back piece, and 1 back from blue gingham. Stitch back to crown/back along all but straight edge. Turn to right side, turn straight edge ¼″ to inside and topstitch all around back. Stitch brims together along all but straight edge; turn to right side and topstitch along curve. Gather raw edge of crown to fit straight edge of brim; stitch together. Cut narrow bias tape in half. Fold each strand lengthwise in half and stitch along center. Tack one end of each to opposite sides of bonnet between brim and back.

*Lamb:* Use pattern to cut 2 bodies (heavy outline all around), 2 underbodies, and 2 ears from black wool; omit seam allowance from ears. Cut a 1½″ × 2⅜″ rectangle from fleece. Stitch bodies together along upper half. Stitch underbodies together for only ¼″ along ends of straight edge. Pin joined underbody to body, matching leg edges. Turn to right side through opening in underbody, stuff firmly, and slip-stitch closed. Glue fleece around body as indicated by dotted lines on pattern. Glue ears to sides of head.

*Assembly:* Dress bear in robe and bonnet. Tack sheep under one arm. Cut twig to approximately 6″ and tack to paw of other arm.

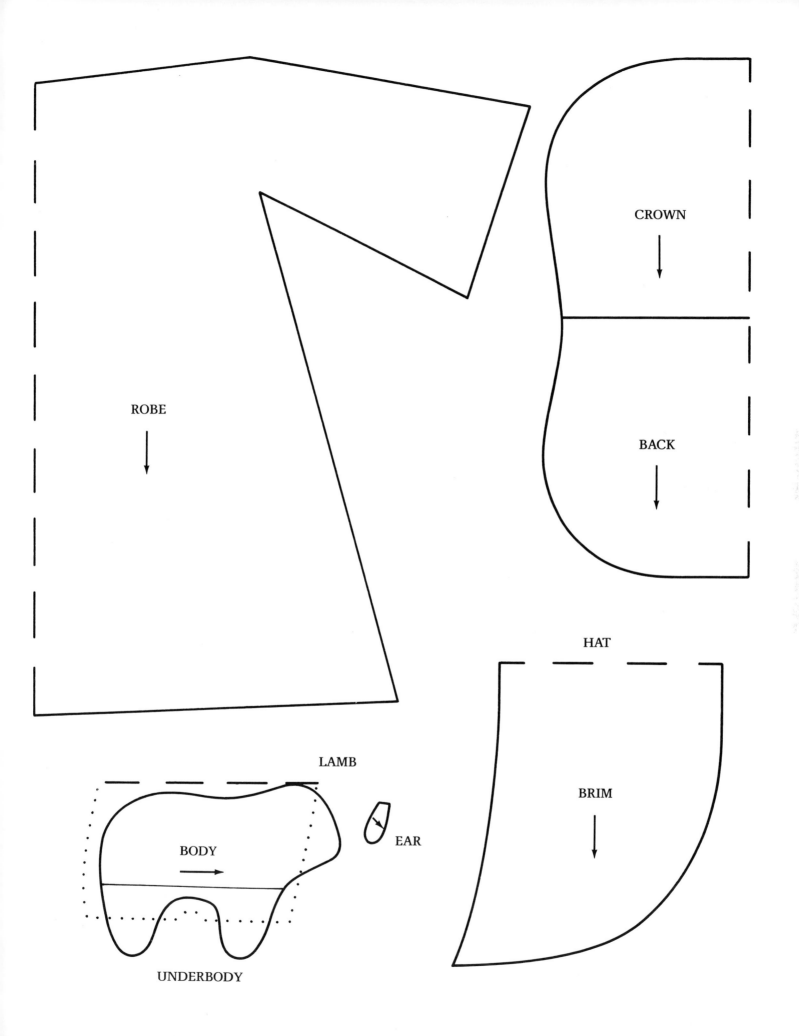

CROWN

BACK

ROBE

HAT

LAMB

BODY

EAR

UNDERBODY

BRIM

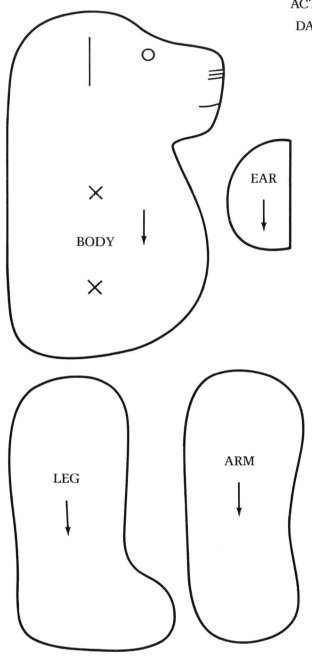

EAR

BODY

LEG

ARM

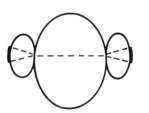

DIAGRAM FOR ARM AND LEG
ASSEMBLY: CROSS-SECTION

# Dassey Bear with Quilt

**Size:** Standing, 5″ tall, seated, 3½″.

**Materials:** Lightweight tan brushed wool fabric 36″ wide, ⅛ yd. White flannel, 6″ square. Scraps of 5 different calico fabrics. Scrap of batting. 2 black 3mm beads. Small amount of tan and black pearl cotton. Polyester fiberfill. Narrow red ribbon, 8″.

**Directions:** *Bear:* Read and refer to "General Directions for Stuffed Animals and Dolls" on page 154. Using

patterns, cut the following from tan wool: 2 bodies, 4 ears, 4 arms, 4 legs.

Stitch pieces together in matching pairs, leaving ½–1″ open along a straight edge. Turn to right side and stuff all but ears firmly with fiberfill. Turn open edges ¼″ to inside and slip-stitch closed. Slip-stitch ears to sides of head. For eyes, stitch one bead to head where indicated by open circle, insert needle through to other side of head and pull thread taut to sink eye. Repeat for other eye. Using a single strand of black pearl cotton, make 5 straight stitches across face for nose, stitch down seam for ¼″ and stitch across for mouth, as shown on pattern.

Attach arms and legs with tan pearl cotton, referring to diagram, which shows a cross-section of body: Beginning at one inside arm, ⅜″ from slightly thicker end (top) and centered between side seams, insert needle through at a slight angle to outside arm. Stitch across arm for ¼″ and return to beginning point. Tie thread to thread end and insert needle through body at point indicated by top X mark on pattern. Continue to stitch through other arm in same manner. Attach legs in same manner, but insert thread ½″ from top of legs and through point on body indicated by bottom X mark.

*Quilt:* Cut 5 calico strips, each 4½″ long and with widths ranging from 1¼″ to 1¾″. Seam strips together along their long edges, then trim to form a 4½″ square. Press seams toward the darker colored fabric. Center patchwork right side up over a 4½″ square of batting and the white flannel backing; pin layers to secure. Using white thread, quilt diagonally across patchwork at 1″ intervals. Turn edges of flannel backing ¼″ then ½″ to quilt top; pin and slip-stitch in place, forming a border.

*Finishing:* Tie ribbon around Dassey Bear's neck. Tack front paws together; pull one corner of quilt between arms.

## Folk Art Oil Paintings: Sheep Farm, Goose Farm

**Sizes:** Each, 16" × 20".

**Materials:** 16" × 20" stretched and pre-primed artist's canvas. Oil paints: Alizarin Crimson (AC), Aqua (A), Burnt Umber (BU), Cadmium Orange (CO), French Ultramarine (FU), Lemon Yellow (LY), Mixed Green (MG), Naples Yellow (NY), Purple (P), Raw Umber (RU), White (W), Yellow Ochre (YO). Turpentine. Clear varnish.

**Equipment:** Paper. Pencil. Graphite paper. Palette. A selection of flat and round tapered paintbrushes.

**General Directions:** Prepare the canvas. If it is not primed, do so by covering canvas with gesso in large flat strokes. Enlarge pattern on a large sheet of paper ruled into 1" squares. Lay pattern on primed canvas with graphite paper in between, and go over design lines lightly with a pencil. As paint is layered onto canvas, concealing design lines, refer to pattern and photograph for details and shading.

Individual directions suggest specific colors for major areas. Paint all surfaces in flat hues first. When paint combinations are indicated, use more of first color of pair or trio mentioned. Next, add shading with darker tones, mixing in a smidge of RU, P, and/or MG. Highlight with lighter tones, by mixing in W and a smidge of NY. Finally, texture with directional brushwork. In general, paint in the dark tones first, followed by the middle tones and then the light tones. Only mix tones where they meet so as not to lose tonal values. Paint the background first, beginning with the sky: use a dark tone of FU + A + W with smidge of P at the top of the paintings, graduating to a very light tone at the horizon by adding W and a smidge of NY. Next, paint the landscape areas behind the animals, and the foreground areas. Lastly, paint the animals themselves. When dry, glaze in three layers with RU, thinned with turpentine, to increase depth and warmth and to give painting the look of age. Apply two thin coats of varnish, letting painting dry thoroughly after each coat.

**Sheep Farm:** Paint sky as indicated in General Directions, add W + LY around the sun, W + CO for sun, the "feather in" clouds of W with a smidge of AC. Paint mountains with W + P. Paint ground and trees with same colors as for *Goose Farm* painting, but keep areas flat, shading only around contours of land and applying brushstrokes of single, unblended color for trees. Use combinations of W, BU, and YO for house, paths, and fences. Paint mountain of foreground with BU + YO and stipple with BU and YO + P + W. Paint sheep with W + NY + BU, pouncing brush with W + BU + CO to add a fleecy texture. Use W + BU + FU to paint hooves, add shade, and shadow. Finally use fine brush and BU + FU to outline body, feet, and facial features, and suggest folds in fleece.

**Goose Farm:** Paint sky as indicated in General Directions, then paint W + P at horizon, for mountains. Paint ground in MG + YO, and make short, up-and-down strokes to simulate grass. Paint trees: BU trunks, various shades of mixed green, FU, and RU for treetops; use wide brushstrokes radiating upward and outward, for the texture of leafy boughs. For geese, paint beaks and feet with YO + CO, paint bodies with W + BU, adding a smidge of A + CO to define wings and shade underbodies. Add BU to all color mixes to add details: nostrils, eyes, wing feathers, and shadows.

PATTERN FOR *SHEEP FARM*    Each square = 1"

131

PATTERN FOR *GOOSE FARM*    Each square = 1″

# Pull-Toy Lamb

*Size:* About 10″ tall, with cart.

*Materials:* Off-white wool bouclé fabric 60″ wide, ¼ yd. 9″ × 12″ square black felt. Green ⅛″-wide suede or grosgrain ribbon, 1¾ yds. Heavy flat lace trim ⅝″ wide: ⅝ yd. each slate blue, sage green, and rose. Sewing thread to match fabrics and laces. Metallic gold embroidery floss. Polyester fiberfill. Dowel ½″ in diameter, 20″ length. Clear pine ½″ × 3⅝″ × 13½″. Black shoe polish. Eight ⅛″ wood screws: four ¾″ long and four 1″ long. Four 6-spoke metal wheels 2½″ in diameter. Four ³⁄₁₆″ × 1″ nails. Twine.

*Directions: Lamb:* Read and refer to "General Directions for Stuffed Animals and Dolls" on page 154. Enlarge patterns, and use as follows: From bouclé fabric, cut 2 each of body, underbody, neck, ear, and tail, omitting seam allowance from curved edges of ears. From felt, cut 2 each of front leg, back leg, and face; cut 4 ears as before.

Stitch necks to bodies from A to B. Matching edges, stack 2 felt ears and top with one bouclé ear, right side up. Topstitch layers together ⅛″ from all edges. At straight edge of each ear, fold in corners ¼″ toward black side; baste in place. Place bouclé side of ear against right side of neck; baste straight edge in place between dots. Stitch faces to necks from C to D, including ears in seams. Stitch darts in underbodies; stitch underbodies together along straight edges. Stitch underbody to body from E to F, leaving bottom of legs open and leaving an opening in one seam for turning. Stitch top edge of bodies together from E to F. Fold each leg piece in half, bringing slanting edges together, and stitch along slant. Turn all pieces right side out. Stuff body firmly. Turn in raw edges of opening and slip-stitch closed. Cut dowel into four 5″ pieces; insert into leg openings in body, leaving about 1¾″ extending.

Pull felt legs over extending dowels, placing wider ends toward body, seams at back, and with lower edges even. Tuck raw edge of bouclé under felt and slip-stitch in place.

Stitch tail pieces together, leaving straight edges open; turn and press. Slip-stitch straight edges to body at marking; tack tail in down position.

*Garland:* Cut a 30″ length of ribbon: mark center point and set aside. Cut remaining ribbon into eleven 3″ lengths.

*Flowers:* Cut all lace into 3″ lengths. Slip-stitch ends of each lace piece together to form a ring, then gather straight edge of lace tightly, forming a rosette. Use six strands of gold floss to make 3 French knots over gathered area for flower center. Beginning at marked center and alternating colors, arrange flowers close together along ribbon; tack in place. To make "leaves," tie on 3″ pieces of ribbon between flowers. Tie garland around lamb's neck.

*Cart:* For axles, cut two ¾″ × 3⅝″ pieces from pine board; sand smooth and set aside. Use cart pattern to trim remaining wood to shape. Drill a ³⁄₁₆″ hole through front of cart at circle. Sand piece smooth. To stain, apply shoe polish to all wood pieces; rub with rags along edges to give a worn look.

Center lamb on bottom side of cart piece with back legs 2⅝″ from back edge; trace around feet. Drill ³⁄₃₂″ holes through cart at center of feet tracings. Place lamb on top side of cart and attach with 1″ screws.

On one ¾″ side of each axle, mark points ⅞″ to either side of center; drill ³⁄₃₂″ holes through axles at points. Place axles on bottom side of cart so

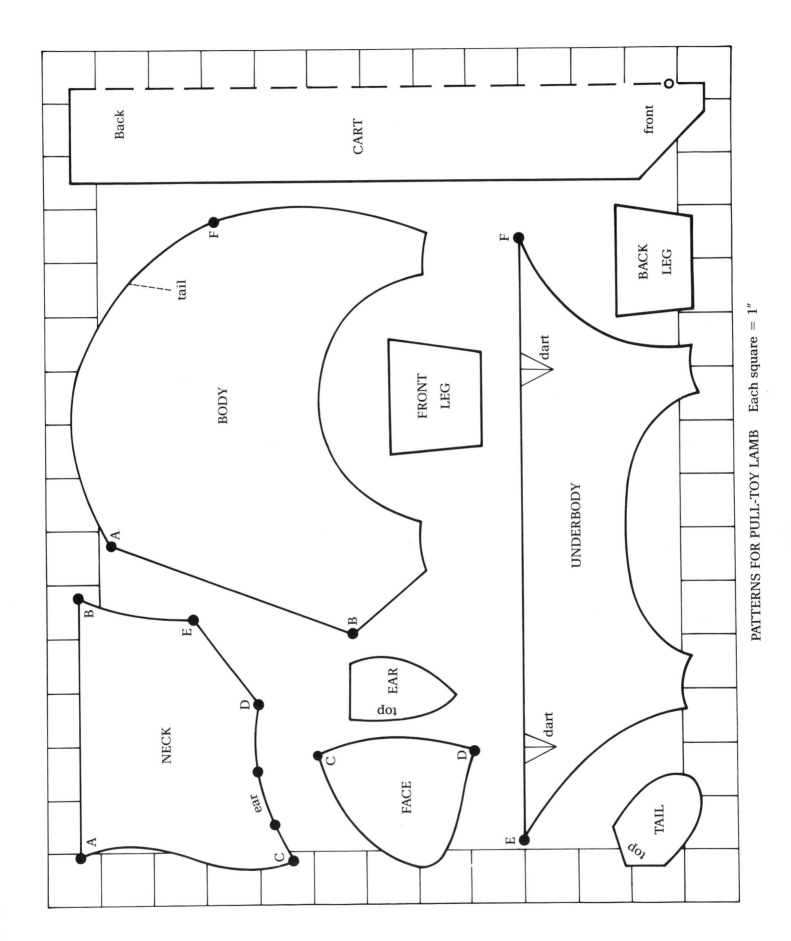

Back

CART

front

BODY

tail

F

A

B

B

E

D

NECK

A

ear

C

FRONT
LEG

F

dart

BACK
LEG

UNDERBODY

EAR

top

FACE

C

D

dart

E

TAIL

top

PATTERNS FOR PULL-TOY LAMB   Each square = 1"

135

that one is 2¾" from front point, the other 1½" from back edge. Attach axles to cart with remaining screws. Attach wheels to ends of axles with nails, allowing a little "play" for wheels to turn easily. Knot one end of a long strand of twine; pass remaining end through hole at front of cart from bottom to top, then knot remaining end.

## Party Horse

*Size:* 19″ tall.

*Materials:* Fabrics: Medium-weight wool (here, brown herringbone) 36″ wide, ⅜ yd.; blue printed cotton 44″–45″ wide, ¼ yd.; small amount of bleached muslin; scrap of blue felt; corner of an embroidered handkerchief or tea towel. Thread to match fabrics. Dark brown six-strand embroidery floss. Satin ribbon scraps: red ¼″, blue 1/16″. Scrap of metallic trim or tinsel. String. Scrap of elastic cord. Two black ¼″ beads. Tiny gold star. Polyester fiberfill. Craft glue.

**Directions:** Read and refer to "General Directions for Stuffed Animals and Dolls" on page 154. Use patterns to cut the following: from wool, 2 heads, 2 torsos, 4 arms, 4 legs; from printed cotton, 2 dress bodices, one $7\frac{1}{4}'' \times 24''$ rectangle, for skirt; from felt, one hat; from muslin, 2 bunny bodies, 4 each ears, arms, legs, plus one $\frac{1}{2}''$ circle, for tail.

*Horse:* Stitch heads, ears, arms, and legs together in pairs, leaving short straight edges unstitched. Stitch torsos together, leaving open at top and bottom edges and between dots along sides. Turn all pieces to right sides. Stuff all but the ears plumply. Turn open edges to inside.

Pinch bottom edge of each ear to form a center pleat and hand-stitch to top of head beside seam. Stitch a bead to one side of head where eye placement is indicated by open circle on pattern. Insert needle through to eye placement on other side, and pull thread taut to sink eye slightly. Stitch other bead in place.

Insert head, with seams centered, into top edge of torso; pin. Insert arms at top sides of torso with seams at top and bottom, thumbs up. Insert legs, with seams centered at front and back, into bottom edge of torso. Slip-stitch all around neck edge, securing head. Slip-stitch limbs in place, stitching through all layers.

*Mane:* Thread floss on embroidery needle. Insert needle into seam at top of head, between ears. Bring to the surface $\frac{1}{16}''$ apart, and tie floss ends in a square knot. Cut ends $\frac{1}{2}''$ from knot. Repeat at seam between eyes, and two more times, evenly spaced, in between.

*Tail:* Cut four $18''$ lengths of floss. Thread each onto needle and stitch through torso back at bottom center. Pull all ends even and tie a knot close to fabric surface. Tie red ribbon around free ends of floss.

*Dress:* Stitch bodices together, leaving open at neck, sleeve ends, and bottom edges. Clean-finish neck edge, hem sleeve ends. Stitch short edges of skirt together to form a ring; gather along one long (top) edge. Pin to bottom edge of bodice with seam at center back; adjust gathers; stitch. Hem bottom edge of skirt.

*Apron:* Cut across a corner of tea towel or handkerchief, $5\frac{1}{2}''$ from point. Stitch a casing along cut edge. Thread an $18''$ length of string through casing for apron strings; knot ends.

*Party Hat:* Bring straight edges of felt hat together and stitch, forming a cone; turn to right side. Tack metallic trim around edge of cone, and glue star to center of hat. Cut a $2\frac{1}{2}''$ length of elastic cord; tack ends to edge of cone at opposite points. Stuff point of hat.

*Bunny:* Stitch body pieces, ears, arms, and legs together in pairs, leaving straight edges open on each. Turn to right side. Stuff ears very slightly, all other pieces firmly. Slip-stitch openings closed. Attach arms to body at upper X-marks, making a cross stitch on outside of one arm, stitching all the way through body and other arm and making a cross stitch on outside of other arm. Repeat with legs at lower X-marks. Stitch ears to top of head. For whiskers, insert three strands of thread through needle; knot $\frac{3}{8}''$ from ends. Stitch through muzzle where indicated by dot on pattern. Fasten off thread close to surface, and cut ends $\frac{3}{8}''$ away. For tail, gather edges of circle, pulling thread ends tight and inserting raw edges to stuff. Stitch to bottom of body across seam. Wrap blue ribbon around neck; tie ends in a bow. If you like, draw a little red heart on inside of one paw with permanent felt-tip pen.

*Assembly:* Slip dress onto horse, and place hat on head. Tack bunny under one arm and tack horse's arms around it.

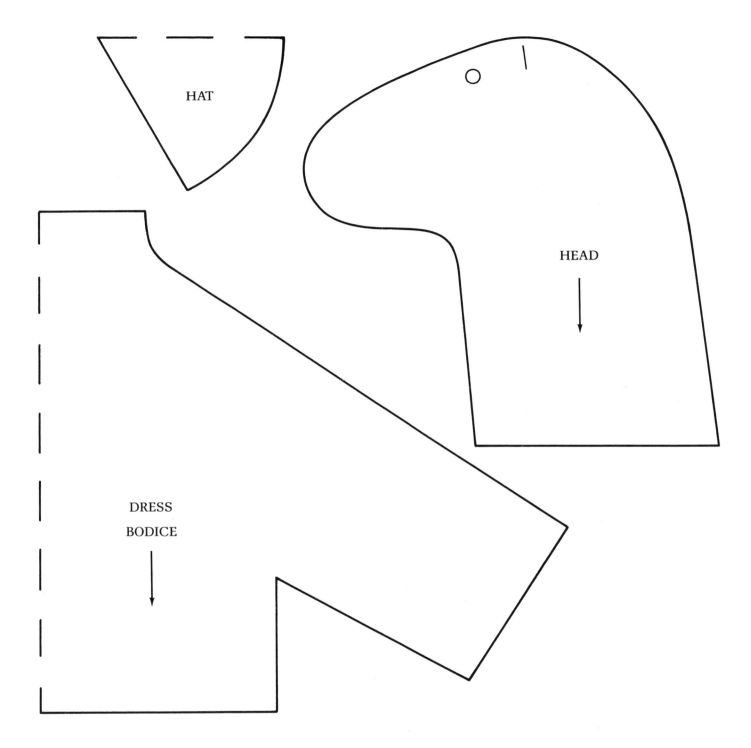

HAT

HEAD

DRESS
BODICE

ACTUAL-SIZE PATTERNS FOR PARTY HORSE

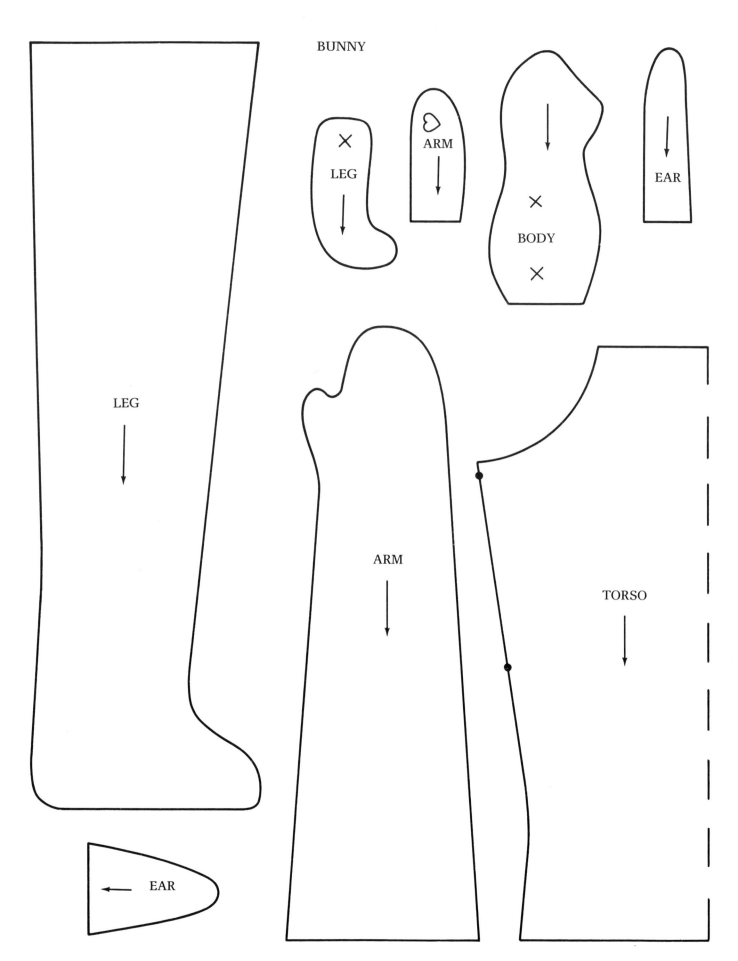

BUNNY

LEG

ARM

BODY

EAR

LEG

ARM

TORSO

EAR

140

## Black Cat

*Size:* 12″ tall.

*Materials:* Cotton fabrics: black sailcloth, 44″–45″ wide, ¼ yd.; one 12″ × 18″ rectangle each blue print, muslin, both "antiqued." Thread to match fabrics. Small amount of gray and blue six-strand embroidery floss. Small amount of white quilting thread. White grosgrain ribbon ¼″ wide, ⅝ yd. Polyester fiberfill.

*Directions:* Read and refer to "General Directions for Stuffed Animals and Dolls" on page 154.

*Cat:* Use patterns to cut the following from black sailcloth: 2 head/bodies, 4 ears, 4 arms, 4 legs.

Embroider face on one head/body piece as follows: Using 4 strands of gray floss, make a French knot for each eye. Using 2 strands of gray floss, straight-stitch eyebrows, and nose, and backstitch mouth. For whiskers, thread one strand of white quilting thread on needle and knot ½″ from end. Insert at one dot, then bring out at another dot. Knot thread close to surface where it emerges and clip thread ½″ from knot. Repeat for second set of whiskers.

Stitch ears, arms, and legs together in pairs, leaving short straight edge open on each. Turn to right side. Pin ears to top edge of head front, side by side with raw edges even. Baste. Stitch head/bodies together, taking care not to catch sides of ears in seams, and leaving bottom edge open. Stuff head/body, arms, and legs, to within 1″ of openings. Close bottom of body like a package: fold sides toward center, then fold front towards the back. Turn raw edge ¼″ to wrong side on remaining back flap, and fold toward the front. Tack in place to secure. Baste across open edges of arms

neckline

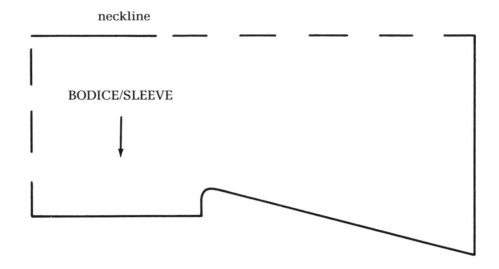

BODICE/SLEEVE

and legs to close, gathering slightly. Stitch to body front as follows: Sew arms 2¼" from top head seam so arms lie horizontally across body, with seams at top and bottom. Sew legs 1" from bottom of body with seams at center front and back.

*Clothing: Dress:* Use pattern to cut a bodice/sleeves from blue printed fabric. Also cut a 7" × 18" rectangle, for skirt. Fold bodice along shoulders and stitch underarm and side seams. Clean-finish neckline and sleeve edges, then gather sleeve edges. Also gather and tack bodice at each end of neckline to create a slight puff at shoulders. Stitch short edges of skirt together, and hem one long (bottom) edge. Gather opposite edge and pin to bottom edge of bodice with seam at center back. Distribute gathers evenly and stitch. Slip dress on doll.

*Bloomers:* From muslin, cut 2 bloomer pieces. Stitch together along sides and inseams. Make a casing at waistline and bottom of each leg. Thread all six strands of blue embroidery floss onto needle. Starting at center front of waistband, insert needle into casing, guide through, and bring out at center front. Leave floss ends 6" long. Repeat at each leg bottom, starting and ending at side seam. Make a knot at end of each strand. Slip bloomers on doll, pull floss ends tight to gather, and tie in bows.

*Apron:* From remaining muslin, cut a 4¼" × 6" rectangle. Clean-finish short (side) edges and one long (bottom) edge. Turn top edge 1" to wrong side, and stitch ¼" from raw edge and again, ¼" from fold. Guide ribbon through casing formed between stitching lines. Gather apron along ribbon, and pull emerging ribbon ends even. Tie apron on doll.

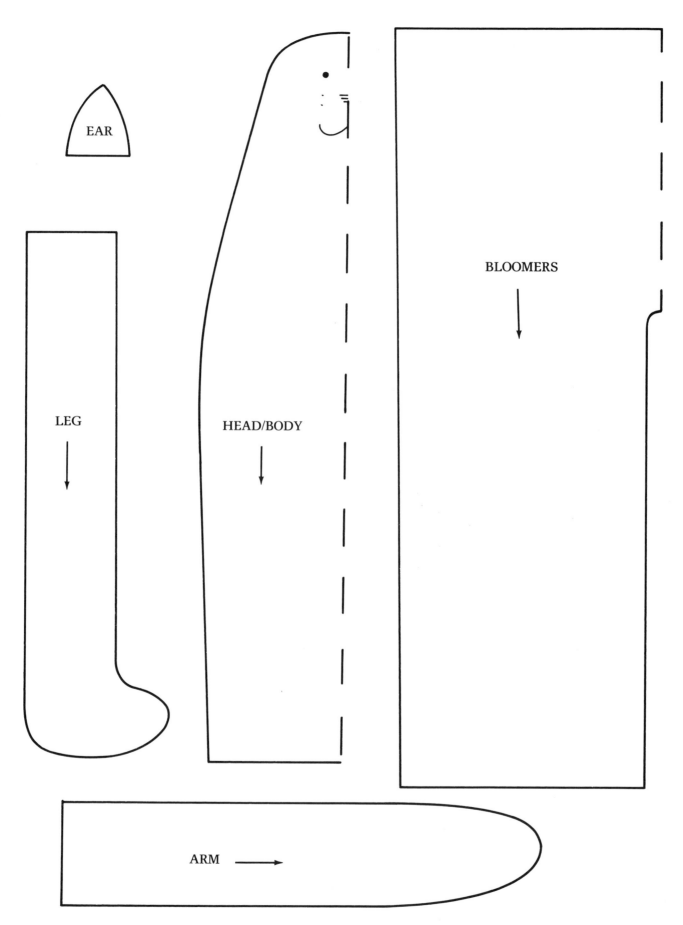

EAR

LEG

HEAD/BODY

BLOOMERS

ARM

## Tea Party Doll Furniture: Table and Chairs

**Sizes:** Trestle table, 1' × 4", 6½" high; chairs, 12" high.

**Materials:** ¾" plywood or pine, two 2' × 4' boards for set. Wood dowel 5⁄16" in diameter, one 36" length per chair. Wood glue. 1¼" finishing nails. Wood filler. Medium oak wood stain.

**Equipment:** Circular saw. Hammer. Sandpaper. Tack cloth. For chairs: Drill with 5⁄16" bit. Coping saw.

**Directions:** Cut pieces with circular saw as directed. Sand smooth. Assemble pieces with wood glue and finishing nails. If desired, countersink nails and apply wood filler to holes. After piece is constructed, stain, rubbing stain well into wood with tack cloth.

*Trestle Table:* From wood, mark and cut the following rectangles: one 1' × 4', for tabletop; two 5½" squares, for upright bases; one 1" × 30", for crosspiece; two 1" × 32", for aprons; four 1" × 5½", for base supports.

Join each end of crosspiece to an upright base, at center of square surface. Centering carefully, glue top edge of uprights to underside of tabletop. Place aprons across top corners of uprights, long edges tight to underside of tabletop. Place base supports along either side of uprights, bottom edges flush.

*Chairs:* For each: From wood, mark and cut the following rectangles: one 6" × 5⅜", for seat; two 1" × 12", for back leg/uprights; two 1" × 2¾", for front legs. From dowel, cut five 5" lengths, two 4" lengths.

Drill ¼"-deep holes: along 1" surface of back leg/uprights, 1½", 3", and 4½" from one (top) end, and 1½" from other (bottom) end; along 1" surface of front legs, 1½" from one (bottom) end. Apply glue to ends of 5" dowels and place between matching pairs of legs, inserting ends into corresponding holes. Let dry. Drill holes on inside ¾" surfaces of each leg, 1" from bottom end. Glue 4" dowels across legs.

With long edges of chair seat at top and bottom, mark a ¾" × 1" rectangle in each upper corner. Use coping saw to cut away marked rectangles. Nail seat over front legs, with cutout areas against back uprights.

## *Vine Wreath with Hearts*

*Size:* Approximately 16" in diameter.

*Materials:* Several long thin branches and vines. A few sprigs of dried flowers or weeds. 10 small wood heart shapes, 2¼" wide, with holes for hanging. Red acrylic paint. Red pearl cotton.

*Directions:* If branches and vines are still green, dry them in the sun for a few days. Denude them of leaves and stems, but leave curly tendrils intact. Soak branches in a tub of water for 10-20 minutes; they should bend without snapping. Twist branches together for about 20", bring ends together and wrap, forming a 16" ring. Soak vines for 2-3 minutes and wrap around entire wreath to secure. Tuck in ends. Let wreath dry.

Paint hearts on one flat surface and side edges; let dry, then paint back. Thread 6" lengths of pearl cotton through holes, and tie hearts, evenly spaced, around wreath. Tuck dried flowers and/or weeds into wreath.

## Gretchen Hooked Rug

*Size:* 36″ × 50″.

Read and refer to "General Directions for Hooked Rugs" on page 153. Mark a center line on burlap, joining long edges. Enlarge pattern on paper ruled into 2″ squares. Place pattern on one half of burlap; align dash line of pattern with marked line; transfer. Reverse pattern to transfer other half, also reversing position of corner motifs as shown. Rug was worked with ¼″-wide strips except for straight inner borders, which are ⅜″ wide. Each flower was worked with one tweed and one solid shade of rose or blue, filling in separate areas as shown. Foliage is solid sage green, light for leaves, medium for stems, dark for ground or vase. All borders are solid maroon. Background is warm beige, in solid but uneven tones.

PATTERN FOR GRETCHEN HOOKED RUG   Each square = 2″

# Epilogue

ew times in the American past has there been such an unabashed love affair with a concept for living such as we are experiencing with American Country. At a time when sophisticated mechanization has created anomie and a yearning for things homemade, it is a welcoming notion that we still can return to a source of the fundamental values borne of our American heritage by bringing the handmade back into our lives.

*American Country Folk Crafts* provides a gateway to our rich craft tradition and all it embodies. I am a quilter, and although I will never grow flax or cotton myself, and I will not prepare, wash, card, or weave the cloth for any bed coverlet, I will, nonetheless, derive from that tradition a spirit—a sense of history—to which old quilts testify. I will don my thimble and carefully wield my threaded needle, as I begin to repeat my quilting stitches across a field of soft-green medallions. My handwork will carry my thoughts through time, where I will take part in the creative spirit from which quilting comes, and the passage of hours will scarcely be felt.

# General Directions ===========

## How to Enlarge Patterns

Because of space limitations, many of the patterns are shown reduced in size. These patterns are presented on a grid, along with a key, such as 1 square = ½" or 1 square = 1".

You will need a sheet of paper large enough to accommodate the full-size pattern—brown paper or taped-together sheets of unlined paper. Using a T- or L-square, draw a rectangle slightly larger than enlarged pattern. Divide rectangle into squares the size indicated by the key. Copy pattern into rectangle, working square by square to correspond.

Or, you can have the pattern Xeroxed at a copy center, enlarging it to the full size.

## Embroidery Stitch Details

Stem Stitch

Chain Stitch

Satin Stitch

Straight Stitch

French Knot

# General Directions for Quilting

**Equipment You Will Need:** Pencil. Tracing paper. Graph paper. Heavy clear vinyl or cardboard and craft glue. Scissors. Straight pins. Sewing and quilting needles. Sewing machine. Dressmaker's tracing (carbon) paper. Iron.

**Marking and Cutting Fabrics:** Use tightly woven cotton or cotton blend fabrics. Wash and dry fabrics to preshrink them; press them thoroughly before marking. Mark fabrics on the wrong side, using a sharp dressmaker's marking pencil. Place all square or rectangular pieces along lengthwise or crosswise grain; ensure right angles by using a ruler, T- or L-square. Mark larger pieces such as quilt backing and borders first, then mark smaller pieces. Mark seam lines on all pieces—dimensions given in instructions include ¼″ seam allowance. Cut out pieces with sharp scissors. All marking and cutting must be done accurately if pieces are to fit together properly.

To avoid confusion, string same type patches together in piles using needle and thread. Remove needle, and lift off patches as needed.

**Making Templates:** Make templates when the same patches or appliqués appear repeatedly. Trace actual-size patterns on clear, heavy plastic, or on tracing paper, which you then glue to lightweight cardboard. When instructions give dimensions only for templates, mark on graph paper, then glue to cardboard. Carefully cut out templates with scissors. To use templates, place them on the wrong side of fabric, and trace around with a sharp pencil or light-colored dressmaker's marking pencil, ¼″ from fabric edges and ½″ apart. Templates do not include seam allowance. Cut out fabric pieces ¼″ outside marked lines.

**Sewing Pieces Together:** Unless otherwise indicated, place pieces together with right sides facing and edges even; make ¼″ seams. For all but square and rectangular patches, stitch only up to and not beyond seam allowance. Unless otherwise indicated, press seams to one side, toward the darker fabric.

**Quilt Assembly:** Lay quilt backing flat on floor, wrong side up; place batting on top. Lay quilt top in place, right side up. Starting at center of quilt, baste to midpoint of all four edges. Starting again at center, baste to four corners. Baste all around edges of quilt top. Trim batting and backing to same size as quilt top.

**Quilting:** Always quilt from the center outwards in all directions. Optimally, place basted quilt in a frame or hoop. Thread a quilting needle with an 18″–24″ length of quilting thread; tie a single knot in end of thread. From front, insert needle through top and batting only, bringing needle up at beginning of quilting line. Tug gently on thread so knot "pops" through top and lodges in batting. Keeping your left hand underneath quilt and right hand on top, work a small running stitch along quilting lines. Make your stitches as small and even as possible. To end off, take a backstitch, insert needle through layers and cut thread at surface—thread end will sink into batting.

# General Directions for Hooked Rugs

**Materials:** Firmly woven wool fabric of medium weight, from remnants, old garments, or blankets; see directions below. Foundation fabric such as open weave (8–10 oz.) burlap, at least 6" wider and longer than finished rug size. Rug binding. Carpet thread.

**Equipment:** Pencil. Ruler and yardstick. Paper for pattern. Dressmaker's tracing (carbon) paper. Straight pins. Masking tape. Dry ball-point pen or tracing wheel. Waterproof marking pen. Large sewing needle. Scissors. Susan Bates 5" straight (or "primitive") rug hook. Optional: Softwood surface. Rug frame. Thumbtacks. Fabric strip cutter, #6 or #8.

**General Directions:** *Pattern:* Enlarge pattern by copying on paper ruled in squares as indicated by keys. Spread burlap foundation fabric on a softwood surface if available; thumbtack edges in place. Otherwise, weight edges with heavy objects to keep burlap from shifting. Place pattern on burlap as directed, aligning with grain; slip carbon between pattern and burlap face down; tape in place. Go over lines of design with tracing wheel or dry ballpoint pen to transfer. Remove pattern and carbon and darken lines of design with waterproof marker.

*Edging:* Hem or bind raw edges of burlap to prevent raveling. Make a line of stay-stitching 1" outside marked outline of rug, using zigzag stitch or backstitching by hand. Before attaching foundation to frame and hooking design, whipstitch one edge of rug binding to edge of marked rug design, using large sewing needle and carpet thread and beginning in center of one side; binding will extend beyond rug design, flat against excess burlap, until hooking is completed.

*Planning Fabric for Hooking:* As a general rule, ½ pound of wool fabric will hook approximately 1 square foot of rug; or, any area to be hooked requires about 4 times its size in wool fabric.

Gather a variety of wool fabrics, combining coarse and fine textures to give character to design. Use solid colors, plaids, tweeds, herringbones, stripes, checks, etc. Avoid hard fabrics such as gabardines or worsteds, very soft fabrics such as cashmere, easily frayed fabrics such as diagonal weaves and knits. Although 100% wool is best, wool blends may occasionally be used for accents. Plan only a few colors for these primitive rugs, although you may want several values and textures of each color. Use muted tones rather than very bright, modern coloring. If you will be using a very dark background, work the design with medium-to-light values; if your background is light, use medium-to-dark values in the design; avoid medium backgrounds. For borders, repeat color(s) used in main design. Shapes are usually filled in with just one color, then outlined in a contrasting color, value, or texture. Work flower centers after rest of rug is completed, when you can choose their colors to complement overall design; avoid repeating background color.

When hooking with used wool fabrics, first wash them well to remove soil, cleaning fluid, and excess dye. Dye fabrics as necessary to achieve desired colors. Cut washed fabric into swatches

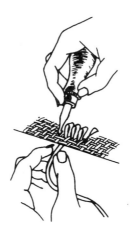

HOOKING DETAIL

6″×12″, then cut swatches in 12″ strips, usually ¼″ wide, cutting either by hand or with a strip cutter. You may wish to cut strips a little narrower (³⁄₁₆″) or a little wider (³⁄₈″), depending on weight of fabric or use in design. If a fabric is thin or loosely woven, cut strips ½″ wide, then fold in half as they are hooked. Cut strips a few at a time, testing that each fabric will pull easily through foundation. Cut swatches and strips on straight of goods, removing selvage and tearing the first inch or so to establish correct cutting line.

*To Hook:* Attach foundation tautly to a frame if desired, following manufacturer's directions; marked design faces up. Before beginning to hook rug, practice making loops in an area outside design. Hold hook above foundation in right hand; hold fabric strip underneath with left hand. Push hook through foundation, catch strip, and pull up a loop about ¼″ high (see detail). Reinsert hook through foundation 2 threads away and pull up another loop. Loops should be close enough together to remain firmly in place, yet far enough apart so rug will not buckle. Continue inserting hook and pulling up loops,

keeping height uniform. When starting and ending a strip, pull ends through to top and clip even with loops. Do not clip loops. Work so that loops in adjacent rows are staggered, or "meshed." Do not pull strips across back of rows.

Work main design first, then fill in background and border (unless you are using a small frame and must complete a section at a time). Start with those elements that appear "on top" or "in front" of the others. For each part of design, work one or more rows of loops around edge, to define shape, then fill in shape with concentric rows where possible, working toward center; avoid straight lines when filling in a curving shape. When design is completed, fill in background in same manner: First work a row of loops around each shape with background color, then continue to fill in, using curved or straight lines as desired; some hookers like to work in small "S" curves.

*Finishing:* Remove rug from frame; turn to back. Trim excess foundation fabric to 1¾″ all around. Turn in raw edge ½″, then turn 1¼″ hem to back of rug, mitering corners; slip-stitch in place. Fold binding to back of rug, covering hem; slip-stitch.

# General Directions for Stuffed Animals and Dolls

*Equipment:* You will need the following items to make the sewn and stuffed projects in this collection: Pencil. Ruler. Tracing paper. Scissors for paper and fabric. Dressmaker's tracing (car-

155

bon) paper in light and dark colors. Dry ball-point pen. Straight pins. Sewing and embroidery needles. Sewing machine. Small knitting needle. Iron.

***Preparing Fabrics:*** Prewash all cotton or cotton blend fabrics to preshrink. To give fabrics an "antique" look, wet fabrics, then soak in tea. Leave fabrics in tea solution for just a few minutes to obtain an overall, light beige tinge. For a mottled effect, spoon a stronger solution of tea over some areas. Let fabric dry, then press on both sides.

***Tracing and Transferring Patterns:*** Enlarge any patterns shown in a grid. Trace actual-size patterns onto tracing paper. Heavy lines indicate pattern outlines and are stitching lines; fine lines indicate embroidery details. Arrows indicate direction of grain. Long dash lines indicate a half (or quarter) pattern. Complete these patterns by tracing pattern twice (or four times) and reversing second (and fourth) tracings. Tape mirror images together along dash lines, and retrace entire pattern.

Pin patterns to the wrong side of fabric designated, placing pieces ½" from fabric edges and ½" apart, with arrows or longest straight edge following the grain. Place dressmaker's tracing (carbon) paper in a contrasting color ink side down in between pattern and fabric. Go over heavy and fine lines and placement markings with a sharp pencil or dry ball-point pen, to transfer patterns to fabric. When more than one piece is needed for a pattern, turn the pattern over to transfer the second and fourth pieces.

***Cutting Pieces:*** Cut out pieces marked from patterns ¼" beyond marked lines for seam allowances. Transfer marked details to right side of fabrics by basting with contrasting thread. For rectangular pieces where measurements but no patterns are given, measure and mark on fabric with longest straight edge along grain. These measurements include seam allowance; cut along marked lines.

***Sewing and Stuffing:*** Pin pieces together with right sides facing and raw edges even, unless indicated otherwise. Machine stitch on marked lines with matching thread, making ¼" seams. Ease in fullness when necessary. Clip into seam allowance along curves and across corners, then turn pieces to their right side. Use a small knitting needle to poke out areas, a pin to lift out tight corners.

*To Stuff:* Shred polyester fiberfill into small pieces, and insert through opening, pushing into far areas and tight corners first. Turn open edges ¼" to inside, and slip-stitch opening closed using matching thread.

*For Clothing:* When assembling pieces, press seams open after stitching.

*To Clean-Finish Edges:* Turn edges ¼" to wrong side and stitch across.

*To Trim Edges with Lace:* Clean-finish edge, cut lace to fit and pin on top, with lace extending past fabric edges. Stitch along bound edge of lace.

*To Gather:* Hand- or machine-baste piece close to edge, leaving thread ends long. Pull basting threads, gathering edge to fit as specified. Adjust gathers evenly or as indicated.

*To Hem:* Turn raw edge ⅛" to wrong side; press. Turn edge another ¼" to wrong side and stitch across, close to first fold line.

*To Make a Casing:* Turn fabric edge ¼", then ½" to wrong side. Stitch close to first fold line. Guide ribbon or string through casing on an embroidery needle or small safety pin.

# Directory of Craftsmen

This Directory is one gateway to the art of craftsmen currently working in the folk-art traditions of the 17th, 18th, and early 19th centuries. It is not a comprehensive compilation, nor is it intended to be. Included are the names and addresses of fine craftsmen with whom I have met and whose work I have admired. A number of names are courtesy of *Early American Life* Magazine, published by Historical Times, Inc., Harrisburg, Pennsylvania. You will happily discover that when you contact any one of these craftsmen, you will be getting in touch with our rich heritage of American folk crafts.

## Baskets

Bryant Holsen Beck
P.O. Box 162
Carboro, NC 27514
Baskets of natural materials:
wild grape, wisteria, and reed;
custom work done on request.

Mr. and Mrs. J.H. Durham
Rt. 2, Box 60
Cherokee, AL 35616
205/ 359-4439
White-oak baskets, some with
natural dyes.

Ross A. Gibson
Day Basket Company
110 W. High Street
North East, MD 21901
301/ 287-6100
Oak baskets; shop open to
visitors.

Sue Gruebel
Log House Primitives
P.O. Box 206
Circleville, OH 43113
614/ 477-1880
Appalachian baskets.

Sue Hahn
Old Times-Baskets
41547 S.R. 558
Leetonia, OH 44431
Natural-brown and dyed-reed
and white-oak baskets; rib,
service, and cheese baskets,
round and square.

Barbara Hala
Bobbie's Baskets
1641 Etta Kable Drive
Beavercreek, OH 45432
513/ 429-3937
Rattan baskets in natural-
walnut dye; traditional
patterns, custom work.

Joe and Sylvia Hemphill
Heritage Baskets
P.O. Box 305
Britton, MI 49229
517/ 451-8500
Stained and colored reeds,
many shapes, including a
tulip basket.

John and Holliday Hays
Holliday and Garshwiler
Rt. 1, Box 34
Bloomingdale, IN 47832
Ribbed-bark, grape-vine,
and splint baskets.

Martha Watson Lorentzen
2 Jared Lane
Yarmouthport, MA 02675
617/ 362-5241
Apple basket, baskets with
dyed loops.

Richard and Jodi McAllister
Red Bird Mission Crafts
HC-69, Box 15
Queen Dale Center
Beverly, KY 40913
606/ 598-2709
Honeysuckle, willow, and
white-oak baskets.

Carol Nelson
Walnut Creek Baskets
12018 217th Street West
P.O. Box 84
Illinois City, IL 61259
309/ 791-0194
Traditional baskets, detailed
weaving.

Donna Rohkohl
The Basket Barn
P.O. Drawer 138
Howell, MI 48843
517/ 546-5316
All kinds of baskets.

Bill and Marilyn Rosenquist
Lightship Baskets
342 Moose Hill Road
Guilford, CT 06437
203/ 453-4512
Nesting baskets.

Alvin and Trevel Wood
2415 East Main Street
Murfreesboro, TN 37130
615/ 895-0391
White-oak baskets,
small and medium sizes.

## Boxes

Gary S. Adriance
Adriance Heritage Collection
5 North Pleasant Street
South Dartmouth, MA 02748
617/ 997-5177
Mahogany, hand-rubbed boxes
in many styles.

Linda Allen
Rt. #4, Box 205
West Brattleboro, VT 05301
Band boxes in many shapes,
covered in wallpaper, lined
with newsprint.

The Friends
Box 464
Frederick, MD 21701
301/ 695-6126
Grained and painted wooden
Shaker boxes.

Lindsay E. Frost
Band Boxes
Box A, Campbell Street
Avella, PA 15312
412/ 587-3990
19th-century boxes: collar,
glove, heart, oval, many sizes.

E.B. Frye and Son, Inc.
Frye's Measure Mill
Wilton, NH 03086
603/ 654-6581
Wooden pantry boxes in
every variety.

Charles Harvey
Simple Gifts
201 C North Broadway
Berea, KY 40403
606/ 986-1653
Shaker boxes made of maple
with solid pine tops and
bottoms, nests of seven,
oiled, stained or painted.

Steven Lalioff
Traditional Leatherwork Company
14311 Bryn Mawr Drive
Noblesville, IN 46060
18th- and 19th-century leather
reproductions, including
trunks, boxes, pouches, and
firebuckets.

Richard and Bess Leaf
Box 223, Rt. 5
Jenkins Chapel Road
Shelbyville, TN 37160
615/ 684-8158
Band boxes with handpainted
paper; wooden boxes, stained
or painted.

Bill Scherer
Shaker Carpenter Shop
8267 Oswego Road
Liverpool, NY 13088
315/ 652-7778
Small items (i.e., spice
chests), furniture.

Jan Switzer
Painted Pony Folk Art
8392 M-72 West
Traverse City, MI 49684
616/ 947-9117
Small wooden chests in
two sizes painted with
Pennsylvania Dutch designs;
other sizes available on
request.

Michelle Worthing
Nancy Yeiser
The Band Box
2173 Woodlawn Circle
Stow, OH 44224
Boxes in many shapes
covered in wallpaper,
lined with newsprint;
will work with custom papers.

## Dolls

Luella Doss
2277 Edgewood Drive
Grafton, WI 53024
414/ 377-9116
Soft-sculpture farm animals in
the folk-art tradition;
barnyard and waterfowl.

Susan Hale
8473 Kaehlers Mill Road
Cedarburg, WI 53012
414/ 377-7393
All fabric, painted canvas-faced
primitive folk dolls and Santas.

Beverly Karcher
60 Dogwood Lane
Watchung, NJ 07060
201/ 754-1812
Folk art primitives in soft
sculpture; custom work accepted.

Tammie Lawrence
Tammie's Teddys
4562 North 77th Street
Milwaukee, WI 53218
414/ 464-0500
Handmade antique replica
teddy bears.

Karen Meer
9110 West Mill Road
Milwaukee, WI 53225
414/ 353-6279
Handmade folk dolls and toys
in soft sculpture; complete
editorial concepts expressed in
animal soft sculpture.

Heidi Steiner
N. 57 W15128 Mesa Drive
Menomonee Falls, WI 53051
414/ 252-3513

Judie Tasch
Original Dolls
3208 Clearview
Austin, TX 78703
512/ 476-5021

## Furniture

Dick Alexander
Yesterday's Yankee
Salisbury, CT 06068
203/ 435-9539
Handcrafted traditional
American furniture;
faithful reproductions
in pine, walnut, maple,
and oak; will accept
custom work.

D.L. Backenstose, Jr.
Spring House Classics
P.O. Box 541
Schaefferstown, PA 17088
717/ 949-3902
Reproductions and
adaptations; custom
work accepted.

David Barrett
Barretts Bottoms
Rt. 2, Box 231
Bower Road
Kearneysville, WV 25430
Ladderback chairs.

Robert Barrow
412 Thames Street
Bristol, RI 02809
401/ 253-4434
Reproduction Windsors.

Michael Camp
636 Starkweather
Plymouth, MI 48170
313/ 459-1190
18th- and 19th-century
reproductions; custom
work accepted.

Steven Cherry
Goshen Mill Road
Peach Bottom, PA 17543
717/ 549-3254
Restorations and
reproductions; custom work
accepted.

Tom McFadden
Star Route 6200
Philo, CA 95466
707/ 895-3627
Handcrafted American furniture.

Thomas Moser
Cabinet Maker
Cobbs Bridge Road
New Gloucester, ME 04260
207/ 926-4446
Custom handmade traditional
American furniture.

Alexandra Pifer
1817 Shoppe, Inc.
5606 East State Rt. 37
Delaware, OH 43015
614/ 369-1817
Upholstered furniture and
country accessories.

David Brian Press
Stonehaven Rt. 312
Brewster, NY 10509
914/ 279-5017
Traditional American
handcrafted furniture.

Jack B. Robinson
8760 Beatty Street, Northwest
Massillon, OH 44646
216/ 832-5641
Mostly custom work in a variety
of woods, paint or stain;
18th-century details including
raised panels, dovetailed joints.

David Sawyer
RD 1, Box 107
East Calais, VT 05650
802/ 456-8836
Reproduction Windsor chairs.

## Iron

Ian Eddy, Blacksmith
RFD 1, Box 975
Putney, VT 05346
802/ 387-5991

Steve Kayne
Kayne and Son Custom Forged
Hardware
76 Daniel Ridge Road
Candler, NC 28715
704/ 667-8868

Charles Lapen, Blacksmith
Rt. 9, Box 529
West Brookfield, MA 01585
617/ 867-3997

Thomas Loose, Blacksmith-
Whitesmith
Rt. 2, Box 2410
Leesport, PA 19533
215/ 926-4849

Ronald Potts, Blacksmith
2255 Manchester Road
North Lawrence, OH 44666
216/ 832-9136

Stephen S. Waligurski and Sons,
Stephen M. and Wayne
Hurley Patentee Lighting
RD 7, Box 98 A
Kingston, NY 12401
914/ 331-5414

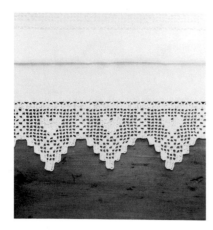

## Needlework

Linda Allen
(Address under "Boxes")
Crochet edging, valences, in antique
patterns and original designs;
custom work accepted.

Nancy Borden
P.O. Box 4381
Portsmouth, NH 03801
603/ 436-4284
Fabric cut and finished
according to a historic
prototype for the period house;
custom bedclothes, hangings,
sheets with monogram and number,
pillow shams and cases, window
treatments, bolster covers,
slipcovers.

Liz Chronister and Kathleen Brock
RD 2
Dillsburg, PA 17019
Samplers made in limited
numbers, framed in old frames
with rippled glass, also
miniature samplers; custom
work accepted.

Elizabeth Creeden
The Sampler
12 North Park Avenue
Plymouth, MA 02360
617/ 746-7077
Traditional crewel including
complete sets of bedhangings;
will also sell finished embroidery,
bargello, and samplers.
Design services available.

Betty Emerson
108 New Haven Road
Oak Ridge, TN 37830
615/ 482-2943
Woven rugs and mats.

Marion N. Ham
Quail Hill Designs
1 Fairview Road
Clark, NJ 07066
-or-
Quail Hill
Limerick, ME 04048
207/ 793-8483
Traditional and primitive
hand-hooked rug patterns
in burlap; offers one-week
live-in workshops in restored
200-year-old farmhouse in
Maine; summer and fall;
accepts custom work.

Caroyl Hart
432 Granite Street
Waupaca, WI 54981
715/ 258-8738
Hooked rugs, limited production;
custom work accepted.

Jean Hipp
Kitnit Needlecrafts
20 Valley Road
Neffsville, PA 17601
717/ 569-3951
Custom knitting, crewel,
needlepoint, bargello.

Pat Hornafius
Lancaster County Folk Art
113 Meadowbrook Lane
Elizabethtown, PA 17022
717/ 367-7706
Hooked rugs; custom work
accepted.

Suzanne C. and Cleland E. Shelby
P.O. Box 201
Essex, VT 05451
802/ 878-4530
Hooked rugs, one-of-a-kind;
limited production; custom orders
accepted.

## Painted Decoration

Donna W. Albro
Strawberry Vine
6677 Hayhurst Street
Worthington, OH 43085
614/ 436-1248
Paint grained boxes, frames,
custom frames, theorem paintings.

Linda Allen
(Address under "Boxes")
Hand-painted wall decorations,
in folk-art and primitive original
designs; custom work accepted.

Phyllis Aycock
1737 York Avenue, Apt. 5M
New York, NY 10028
212/ 860-5526
Custom portraits in primitive
style; reproduction antique
portraits, still lifes, land- and seascapes.

Sandra Buck
Buck Mountain Stenciling
Maple Corner
Calais, VT 05648
802/ 229-9326
Floorcloths stenciled in original
designs adapted from early American
quilts and stenciling.

Philip and Nancy Cayford
Good and Co. Floorclothmakers
Salzburg Square, Rt. 101
Amherst, NH 03031
603/ 672-0490
Reproduction and original
floorcloth designs.

Peter Deen
Goshen Mill Rd.
Peach Bottom, PA 17563
717/ 548-3254
Restoration and reproduction
paint on furniture; techniques
for making paint look old and
matching colors.

Pamela Friend
590 King Street
Hanover, MA 02339
617/ 878-7596
Primitive paintings on
canvas, wall, fabric, and
floor stenciling; custom work
accepted.

Elizabeth F. Gilkey
3625 Stettinus Avenue
Cincinnati, OH 45208
513/ 871-4077
Primitive oils, farm animals,
landscapes, portraits; custom
work accepted.

David and Marie Gottshall
Gottshall's Folk Art
210 East High Street
Womelsdorf, PA 19567
215/ 589-5239
Mostly custom work, graining
new and antique furniture,
reverse painting on glass,
house restoration.

Christopher Gurshin
Itinerant Painter
P.O. Box 616
Newburyport, MA 01950
617/ 462-7761
Original works include on-site
decorative painting, primitive
and traditional murals,
stenciling, and small oil paintings;
painted pine houses and animals,
and decorated stationery.

Dorothy Wood Hamblett
P.O. Box 295
Millbury, MA 01527
Teaches painted decoration
to groups on location and by
correspondence; marbleizing,
graining, stenciling on wood and
walls. Member of HSEAD, Inc.

Claudia and Carroll J. Hopf
13 Mechanic Street
Kennebunk, ME 04043
207/ 985-4654
Fancy grained wooden wares,
scherenschnitte.

The Jersey Limner
1 Fairview Road
Clark, NJ 07066
201/ 388-8611
Museum-quality naive folk paintings
and murals of distinction. Commissioned
oils on canvas characterizing people,
animals, or estates in primitive fashion.
Period landscape wall murals in the
Porter style. Work from photographs;
preliminary sketches provided on request.

Gladys Daniels Johnston
Box 151
Wayne, IL 60184
312/ 584-2491
Floorcloths, almost exclusively
custom work.

Tom Kelly
3 Liberty Street
Mineral Point, WI 53565
608/ 987-2295
Reproduction frakturs, grained frames,
fireboards, and folk sculptures.

Sherry Mason
Olde Virginia Floorcloth
and Trading Co.
P.O. Box 3305
Portsmouth, VA 23701
804/ 393-0095
Custom floorcloths in
sizes $2' \times 3'$ to $8' \times 10'$;
makes pencil post beds.

Megan Parry
1727 Spruce
Boulder, CO
303/ 444-2724
Wall stenciling and mural services;
custom work accepted.

Maggie Schuchardt
909 Progressive Lane
Monona, WI 53716
608/ 222-8197
Hand-stenciling; folk-art painting
and three-dimensional folk-art
paintings depicting scenes from
country life.

Roberta Taylor
1717 Maywood Drive
West Lafayette, IN 47906
317/ 497-3111
Fancy painting on any surface;
Santa figures.

David Bradstreet Wiggins
Itinerant Painter
Hale Road, Box 420
Tilton, NH 03276
603/ 286-3046
Original period interior murals,
marbling, graining; designer and
decorator of individual rooms;
slide show and discussion available
for consulting fee. Travel affects fee.

Marjorie S. Yoder
North Street, Box 181
Morgantown, PA 19543
215/ 286-5490
Hand-stenciled table linens.

## Pewter

S. Barrie Cliff
Pewter Crafters of Cape Cod
927 Main Street Route 6A
Yarmouthport, MA 02675
617/ 362-3407

Lydia Holmes
Pilgrim Pewterers
Stow, MA 01775
617/ 568-8838
Spoons and buttons made with
antique molds.

J. Thomas Stauffer
707 West Brubaker Valley Road
Lititz, PA 17543-0707
717/ 626-7067

David Weber
Village Pewter
320 West Washington Street
Medina, OH 44256
216/ 725-8545

## Pottery

Melinda Ashley-Masi
16 Savin Avenue
Norwood, MA 02062
617/ 769-6321
Porcelain bowls, vases, platters,
painted floral decorations.

Bastine Pottery
R.R. 3, Box 111
Noblesville, IN 46060
317/ 776-0210
Stoneware with cobalt-blue spatter-
decorated with farm animals.

Heather and Jack Beauchamp
Salt O'Thee Earth Pottery
71456 Bates Road
Guernsey, OH 43741
614/ 439-1936
Stoneware with cobalt decorations.

Gerard T. Beaumont
Beaumont Pottery
293 Beech Ridge Road
York, ME 03909
207/ 363-5878
Salt-glazed stoneware with
handpainted cobalt-blue designs

Lester Breininger
Breininger's Pottery
476 South Church Street
Robesonia, PA 19551
Reproduction Pennsylvania
German redware.

Anne Burnham and Gary Quirk Potters
Star Route/Picketville Road
Parishville, NY 13672
315/ 265-3175
Hand-built and thrown stoneware
porcelain.

David Elreth
4351 Forge Road
Nottingham, PA 19362
Salt-glazed stoneware with
cobalt decorations.

David and Mary Farrell, Potters
Westmoore Pottery
Rt. 2, Box 494
Seagrove, NC 27341
919/ 464-3700
Salt-glazed stoneware and
Moravian pottery.

Carl Ned Foltz
The Foltz Pottery,
Pennsylvania Redware
RD #1, Box 131
Peartown Road
Reinholds, PA 17569
215/ 267-3016
Redware with slip decoration.

Tim Galligan and Kathy Kellagher
Star Rt., Box 155
Marienville, PA 16239
814/ 927-8410
Salt-glazed stoneware with brushed
cobalt-blue designs.

Gris Potter
111 West Main Street
Dundee, IL 60118
312/ 428-4747
Country redware.

Charlotte Lee Helsley
Lee-Ware
525 Waterville Road
Avon, CT 06001
203/ 678-9178
10"-diameter porcelain bowls

Debra and Joel Huntley
Wisconsin Pottery
R.R. 1, Box 219
Columbus, WI 53925
414/ 992-5242
Salt-glazed stoneware.

Jensen Turnage Pottery
8529 Hicks Island
Lanexa, VA 23089
804/ 566-1989
Potters for Colonial
Williamsburg; also makes a
line of handpainted, delicate
porcelain.

Jan Lacoste
40 Stow Street
Concord, MA 01742
617/ 369-0278
Porcelain influenced by English delft,
French, and Chinese antiques;
custom work accepted.

The Long Family Potters
Old Eagle Studios
237 Bridge Street
Phoenixville, PA 19460
215/ 933-3080
Redware, early English delft
reproductions, dinnerware made
to order.

Diana McClure
McClure Pottery
5409 Lester Lane
Cincinnati, OH 45213
513/ 531-6366
Colanders, blue-and-white pottery.

Becky Mummert
30 Fish and Game Road
East Berlin, PA 17316
717/ 259-9620
Cobalt-decorated stoneware and
Pennsylvania redware.

David T. Smith
Turtlecreek Potters
3600 Shawhan Road
Morrow, OH 45212
513/ 932-2472
Museum-quality redware reproductions
that look old; tableware and sliptrail
decoration; great variety.

L. L. Szymborski
1505 Geyers Church Road
Middletown, PA 17057
717/ 944-5445
Earthenware and reproduction delft,
green-and-blue chargers;
custom work accepted.

## Textiles

Nancy Borden
P.O. Box 4381
Portsmouth, NH 03801
603/ 436-4284
$10 brochure includes color photos of
work in room settings, historical references, glossary of terms; offers whole
scope of period fabric and scholarly
consultation for replicating historically
accurate textile items in context. Fabrics include handwoven stripe carpet-
ing, linen check, linsey woolsey,
domestic linens, and manufactured
museum reproduction prints. Sells fabric by the yard. Most work includes travel for on-site consultation to determine
historical precedent.

Betsy Bourdon, Weaver
Schribner Hill
Wolcott, VT 05680
802/ 472-6508
Blankets, rag rugs, linens.

Diane Jackson Cole, Handweaver
9 Grove Street
Kennebunk, ME 04043
207/ 985-7387
Woven fibers, predominantly natural
ones (silk, wool, cotton, cashmere,
linen); creates throws and apparel.

Laura A. Copenhaver
"Rosemont"
P.O. Box 149
Marion, VA 24354
703/ 783-4663
Coverlets, quilts, canopies.

Sandi Dobson
115 Beaumont Street
Brooklyn, NY 11235
718/ 934-6858
Quilts and quilt-piece pillows.

Janice L. Ebert
Traditional Handweaver
4375 South Kessler-Frederick Road
West Milton, OH 45383
513/ 698-6986, evenings
Reproduction weaving; wool rugs
in checks, plaids, stripes; rag
rugs; linens; throws; custom
work accepted.

Susan Eikenberry
611 North Van Buren Street
Batavia, IL 60510
312/ 879-7259
Overshot coverlets;
custom work accepted.

William A. Leinbach
The Itinerant Weaver
356 Royers Road
Myerstown, PA 17067
717/ 866-5525
Coverlets in many colors.

Ellen Leone
Plain and Fancy
RD 2, Box 450
Bristol, VT 05443
802/ 453-3315
Linen and cotton blend towels,
placemats, tablerunners, and napkins;
wool blankets, stripes and
window-pane plaids.

Julia A. Lindsey
Lindsey Woolseys of Ohio
275 North Main Street
Germantown, OH 45327
513/ 855-6424
Coverlets, pillows, rugs.

Kay Marshall
2201 Anton Way
Anchorage, AK 99503
907/ 276-4932
Handmade wool blankets.

Donna Nedeeisky, Handweaver
P.O. Box 02-616
Portland, OR 97202
503/ 771-5949
Handwoven reproduction coverlets
and information about proper storage
of old coverlets; sells spinning
equipment and teaches spinning
and dyeing.

Pat Nolan
The Rug House
1437 Herschel Avenue
Cincinnati, OH 45208
513/ 871-0890
Braided and woven rugs;
custom work accepted.

Tim and Maureen Rastetter
Rastetter Woolen Mill
Star Route
Millersburg, OH 44654
216/ 674-2103
Handmade wool and goosedown
comforters and feather bedding.

Martha Richard
The Weaver's Corner
1406 East Spring Street
New Albany, IN 47150
812/ 948-0350
Cotton rag rugs, large and small
sizes; custom work accepted.

Rebecca Francis Weaver
Box 307
Dillsburg, PA 17019
Authentic wool rag rugs.

Mary Worley
Traditional Textiles
RD 2, Box 3120
Middlebury, VT 05735
802/ 462-2315
Mostly custom work, coverlets,
blankets, toweling made on antique
equipment with natural dyes.

# Tin

David Claggett, Tinsmith
3N041 Woodview Drive
West Chicago, IL 60185
Reproductions of tin lighting
and odd, authentic 18th-century
folk art.

K. Claggett, Tinsmith
RD #3, Box 330-A
Quarryville, PA 17566
717/ 786-8249
Reproduction lighting, cookie
cutters, cut-outs; custom work
accepted.

Jim DeCurtins
Tin Peddler
203 East Main Street
Troy, OH 45373
513/ 335-2231
Handcrafted lighting.

The Tin Man by Gerald Fellers
2025 Seneca Drive
Troy, OH 45373
513/ 339-8164
Reproduction tin lighting,
pierced panels for pie safes,
candle boxes.

Robert and Sylvia Gerlach
Gerlachs of Lecha
P.O. Box 213
Emmaus, PA 18049
Cookie cutters in large variety.

Mary Gillaspy, Native Crafts
Dawson Gillaspy, Tinsmith
Covered Bridge Road
RD 2, Box 312
Oley, PA 19547
215/ 689-4227
Household items, sconces,
lighting.

Robert and Anita Horwood
Horwood's Country House
4037 Gotfredson Road
Plymouth, MI 48170
313/ 453-8659
Reproduction tin for the kitchen,
reflector ovens, roasters, lighting.

Charles R. Messner
Colonial Lighting and Tinware
Reproductions
316 Franklin Street
Denver, PA 17517
215/ 267-6295
Custom work for farms
and individual clients;
stovepipes, bakery trays, and
sconces.

Mark Rocheford, Thomas Savriol
Lighting by Hammerworks
75 Webster Street
Worcester, MA 01603
617/ 755-3434
Colonial reproduction lighting
and accessories, lanterns,
sconces, forged hardware; custom work
accepted; also works in iron,
copper, and brass.

# Wax

Pat and Jack Briggs
Candlewick
P.O. Box 366
Portland, MI 48875
517/ 647-6694
Fine hand-dipped candles in
the American tradition,
twenty colors.

Katie Fross
RR 2, Box 531
Momensce, IL 60954
815/ 472-6783
Molded beeswax ornaments;
molds are antique chocolate
and ice-cream molds: hearts,
trees, doves, Father Christmas;
sizes vary from 1″ × 1″ to 10″ × 13″.

S. and C. Huber
82 Plants Dam Road
East Lyme, CT 06333
203/ 739-0772
Hand-dipped candles.

Becky Rupp
Candles and Co.
Box 144
Brandamore, PA 19316
Molded, scented candles,
many colors.

The Shoemakers
RD #2, Box 212A
Oley, PA 19547
215/ 689-5022
Hand-dipped candles.

Cliff and Lois Sunflower
Bear Honey Farms
2371 West Best Road
Bath, PA 18014
215/ 759-9655
Beeswax candles, ornaments,
bulk wax, and honey.

## Wood Sculpture (or Carving)

Charles and Linda Detweiler
Detweiler Folk Art
P.O. Box 2883
Sherman, TX 75090
241/ 868-1088
Constructs quilt designs
in wood; suitable for framing.

Harold B. Goebel
2292 Edgewood Drive
Grafton, WI 53024
414/ 377-2016
Folk-art farm animals in wood:
pull-toy pigs, standing and sitting;
rocking horses, pull-toy rooster
16″–18″.

David Ritter
101 North Haggin
P.O. Box 2108
Red Lodge, MT 59068
406/ 446-1227
Hand-carved ducks and geese.

LeRoy Zeigler
9110 West Mill Road
Milwaukee, WI 53225
414/ 353-6279
Hand-carved folk sculpture;
custom orders accepted.

## Miscellany

Ivan Barnett
RD 1
Stevens, PA 17578
717/ 738-1590
Original handcrafted weather vanes;
custom work on request.

Michael Bonne, Coppersmith
Michael and Teresa Bonne
RR 1, Box 177
Carthage, IN 46115
317/ 565-6521

James Chamberlain
Colony Brass
P.O. Box 266
Williamsburg, VA 23187
804/ 898-2942

Clocks by Foster Campos
213 Shoosett Street
Pembroke, MA 02359
617/ 826-8577
Museum quality reproduction
clocks with weight-driven
works.

Robin Lankford
Folk Hearts
15005 Howe Road
Portland, MI 48875
517/ 647-6298
Gameboards and folk-art figures.

Joe Panzarella and
Jane Byrne Panzarella
High Point Crafts
RD 2/Sky High Road
Tully, NY 13159
315/ 696-8540
Woven fireplace brooms; Shaker style.

Virginia Petty
The Whistlin' Whittler
1684 Three Forks Flat
Rock Road
Oakland, KY 42159
Wooden spoons and other
wooden objects.

Ken Ratcliff
Ratcliff String Instruments
107 North Wilson Avenue
Morehead, KY 40351
606/ 783-1111
Handmade instruments and repairs;
violins, mandolins, guitars and
dulcimers.

JoAnne Schiavone
Schiavone Books
60 Itaska Place
Oceanport, NJ 07757
201/ 222-7644
Marbleized covers, folded
handmade paper inside, coptic
bindings, table screens.

## Museums

Many museums across the nation offer
handmade, high-quality reproductions
and adaptations of pieces in their
collections.

# Acknowledgments

his book, which celebrates the creative process, was made possible through the expertise, commitment, and kindness of many creative people. I would like to express my thanks and appreciation to the craft designers and the bakers who enthusiastically shared their unique creations; to Eleanor Levie, writer of the directions, whose professionalism and ever-present support made an overwhelming task achievable; to Charlotte Biro, who wrote the directions for the crochet projects; to Roberta Weiss Frauwirth, whose patterns and illustrations added an unexpected aesthetic dimension to this book.

I am also grateful to Virginia and John Gray, Kathy Lichter and Steve Zazula, Gloria Smith, and Jane and William Grainger, whose homes were graciously opened to us and whose personal collections of antiques were unselfishly loaned. Special thanks to these friends who helped behind the scenes: Gloria Smith of Yankee Peddler Antiques & Workshop, Huntington, New York; Cynthia Beneduce of Cynthia Beneduce Antiques, New York, New York; Urte Tuerpe of Village Flowers, Huntington, New York; and especially Tracey McCauley, Maryann Pettit, Heather Tucker, Ceil Rossi, Bonnie Williamson, Lisa Witschi, and Christina Haskin, who recognized and encouraged me throughout—knowing all of you were there made all the difference in the world.

In particular, I wish to thank Kathy Lichter for affirming the essence of "country" with the seamless styling; her tireless enthusiasm, her creative energy, and her generous hospitality were remarkable and appreciated. Joe Eck arranged the flowers and natural materials in an inspiring way; his creations appear in the kitchen, living room, and master bedroom chapters.

For Beth Galton and her photography, I have only appreciation and respect; Beth's photographic vision aligned so perfectly with my highest aspirations for this book that every reader can now experience the full impact of each folk craft. Alex Lippisch and David Massey assisted in the photography with skill and sensitivity.

I am indebted to my editor, Lois Brown, whose editing and support were always skillful and diplomatic; and to Rebecca Wolcott Atwater, who assisted in the early stages of editing the material on quilts. I want to thank Sam Antupit for his enthusiasm for the project and Darilyn Lowe for her elegant design of the book.

Finally, my love and thanks to my husband, John, and our great kids, Genevieve, Rodney, and Gabrielle, who stood by me through the long months (day and night) of research, designing, travel, and writing.

# Bibliography

## Books

Bath, Virginia Churchill. *Needlework in America: History, Designs, and Techniques.* New York: Viking Press, 1979.

Bishop, Robert and Patricia Coblentz. *A Gallery of American Weathervanes and Whirligigs.* New York: E.P. Dutton, 1981.

Bishop, Robert, William Secord, and Judith Reiter Weissman. *Quilts, with Coverlets, Rugs & Samplers.* New York: Alfred A. Knopf, 1982.

Bishop, Robert, Judith Reiter Weissman, Michael McManus, and Henry Nieman. *Folk Art, Paintings, Sculpture & Country Objects.* New York: Alfred A. Knopf, 1983.

Brant, Sandra and Elissa Cullman. *Small Folk; A Celebration of Childhood in America.* New York: Dutton in Association with The Museum of American Folk Art, 1980.

Emmerling, Mary Ellisor. *American Country, A Style and Source Book.* New York: Clarkson N. Potter, Inc., 1980.

Fox, Sandi. *Small Endearments, 19th-Century Quilts for Children.* New York: Charles Scribner's Sons, 1985.

Guilland, Harold F. *Early American Folk Pottery.* Philadelphia, PA: Chilton Book Company, 1971.

James, Michael. *The Quiltmaker's Handbook, A Guide to Design and Construction.* Englewood Cliffs, NJ: Prentice-Hall, Inc., 1978.

Lichten, Frances. *Folk Art of Rural Pennsylvania.* New York: Charles Scribner's Sons, 1946.

Mills, Susan Winter. *Illustrated Index to Traditional American Quilt Patterns.* New York: Arco Publishing, Inc., 1980.

Morton, Robert. *Southern Antiques & Folk Art.* Birmingham, AL: Oxmoor House, Inc., 1976.

Peto, Florence. *American Quilts and Coverlets.* New York: Chanticleer Press, 1949.

Peto, Florence. *Historic Quilts.* New York: The American Historical Company, Inc., 1939.

Robacker, Earl F. *Old Stuff in Up-Country Pennsylvania.* South Brunswick and New York: A.S. Barnes and Company, 1973.

Schaffner, Cynthia V.A. and Susan Klein. *Folk Hearts, A Celebration of the Heart Motif in American Folk Art.* New York: Alfred A. Knopf, 1984.

Smith, Carter. *Decorating with Americana; How to Know Where to Find It, and How to Make It Work For You.* Birmingham, AL: Oxmoor House, Inc., 1985.

Thuro, Catherine M. *Primitives & Folk Art, Our Handmade Heritage.* Paducah, KY: Collector Books, 1979.

Walters, James. *Crochet Workshop.* London: Sidgwick & Jackson, 1979.

Wamsley, James S. *The Crafts of Williamsburg.* Williamsburg, VA: The Colonial Williamsburg Foundation, 1982.

## Pamphlets

"Frances A. Clapp Sampler–1836; McCall's Heritage Collection." New York: ABC Needlework & Crafts Magazines, Inc., 1984.

# Biography of the Author

Carol Endler Sterbenz has admired, collected, and designed American Country folk crafts for many years. She is author of the best-selling *The Gnomes Book of Christmas Crafts* and co-author of *The Decorated Tree*, both published by Abrams. Ms. Sterbenz has written and illustrated several books for children as well.

A frequent contributor to *McCall's Needlework & Crafts* Magazine, she was the Creative Director of their Special Activities Division. Her designs are in several private collections and in The Museum of the City of New York. Carol Sterbenz resides in Huntington Bay, New York, with her husband, John, and their three children, and currently she is at work on a book about the regional handcrafts of France.

# Index of Folk Crafts in This Collection